3-18-76

THE READER'S GUIDE TO PROCLAMATION

TO PROCLAMATION

Cycle "B"

THE READER'S GUIDE
TO PROCLAMATION

For Sundays and Major Feasts
in Cycle "B"

by Jerome J. DuCharme

FRANCISCAN HERALD PRESS
CHICAGO, ILLINOIS 60609

Library of Congress Cataloging in Publication Data

DuCharme, Jerome J

The reader's guide to proclamation for Sundays and
major feasts in cycle "B".

1. Bible—Liturgical lessons, English. 2. Bible—Liturgical use. I. Title.

BS391.2.D83   264'.0203   75-26816

ISBN 0-8199-0578-X

Published With Ecclesiastical Approval
MADE IN THE UNITED STATES OF AMERICA

Dedicated to our two sons
Larry and Paul
whom Gail and I touch
with our love

ACKNOWLEDGEMENTS

I wish to express my gratitude to Father Mark Hegener, Managing Director of Franciscan Herald Press, who encouraged me by believing in my ability to write this book. I also want to thank Jim Wilbur and Father Dan Coughlin for their advice, support and friendship.

INTRODUCTION

I am pleased to have another opportunity to share my reflections on the Scripture readings for Sundays and major feasts. The commentaries in this book are intended as a sharing by a believer with other believers, with the hope that we will proclaim the Scriptures with greater enthusiasm, with growing faith in God's Word and deeper reverence for God's people. Like the Cycle A book, *THE READER'S GUIDE TO PROCLAMATION* for Cycle B is non-technical in content and approach.

How may *THE READER'S GUIDE TO PROCLAMATION* be used? I recommend that the reader begins in a prayerful, reflective way. Read slowly through the first two readings and the gospel. Read the commentary in *The Reader's Guide to Proclamation.* Then reread the scriptural texts, followed by a second reading of the comments. Try to see other connections and meanings which may not be suggested in the comments. Next comes the important practice session. If possible, this practice should take place at the lectern with the use of the microphone. The "buddy" system in which two or more readers help each other by listening and giving critiques has many advantages. Throughout the entire preparation, there is the need to be prayerful.

There is no easy way to become a more effective reader. The preparation for each set of readings requires time, work, study and prayer. Being a reader means to be willing to serve the people, because the reader is a minister of the Word. When we proclaim the Scriptures, we invite God's people to celebration. The Liturgy of the Word (the three readings and the homily) prepares us to encounter the risen Jesus, present and active among us as we pray the Eucharist.

Since the first two readings are usually connected with the gospel in a unified theme, it is important in

Cycle B to focus our attention on the gospel of Mark. Mark, the most frequently occurring gospel in this cycle, is challenging and refreshing.

One of Mark's characteristics is the "Messianic Secret," Jesus' attempt to conceal his own identity. Because many people quickly misinterpreted whatever Jesus said and did, he had to be extremely cautious. We often read how Jesus asked his followers and the people whom he cured not to reveal his identity. Only in their faith experience of the risen Lord would the disciples of Jesus better understand his words and actions. After the Transfiguration, Jesus "strictly enjoined them not to tell anyone what they had seen, before the Son of Man had risen from the dead. They kept this word of his to themselves, though they continued to discuss what 'to rise from the dead' meant" (Mk 9:9–10).

When Mark wrote his gospel, years after Jesus' death and Resurrection, he believed in the risen Jesus. And so in the gospel of Mark, Jesus' prohibition not to reveal his own identity "before the Son of Man had risen from the dead" (Mk 9:9) may well be a disguised invitation to the early Christians and ourselves to discover through the gospel the risen Jesus in our midst. Isn't this what occurs in the gospel passages? "A leper approached him. . . . Moved with pity, Jesus stretched out his hand. . . . Jesus gave him a stern warning and sent him on his way. 'Not a word to anyone, now'. . . . The man went off and began to proclaim the whole matter freely, making the story public" (Mk 1:40, 41, 43, 44, 45). "He enjoined them strictly not to tell anyone; but the more he ordered them not to, the more they proclaimed it" (Mk 7:36).

Mark wrote his gospel for communities of early Christians who came to know the risen Lord in the proclaimed Word and in their experience of the breaking of bread. Certain passages suggest to us that Mark intended his gospel to be savored in a Eucharistic setting. He frequently describes Eucharistic attitudes: "The people were spellbound" (Mk 1:22). "All who looked on were amazed" (Mk 1:27). "They were awestruck; all gave praise to God, saying, 'We have never seen anything like this!' " (Mk 2:12) "A great awe overcame them" (Mk 4:41). "They were all amazed at what they heard" (Mk 5:20). "At this the family's astonishment knew no bounds" (Mk 5:42).

In our attempts to lead the people to the Eucharist through a stirring proclamation of the Word, we must acknowledge a "hang-up" which many of us have. As children we were discouraged when we tried to express negative emotions: "Don't be angry. . . . You shouldn't be jealous. . . . Don't be afraid!" Men especially were told to conceal sadness and disappointment: "Boys don't cry." Since we have made a lifelong effort to suppress negative emotions, many of us consequently have difficulty expressing the positive emotions which are necessary in the enthusiastic proclamation of Scripture. We guard against showing real enthusiasm in public. We hold ourselves back.

Why not allow ourselves to be surprised by the love which God shows for us in Jesus? Why not react openly before our brothers and sisters in a genuine spirit of proclamation? When we proclaim God's Word freely, we will discover how the Word prepares us and leads us to a joy-filled celebration of the Eucharist. In our Eucharistic prayer we will become more aware of the continuing, dynamic presence of Jesus among us. I pray that in using *THE READER'S GUIDE TO PROCLAMATION* lay readers and all who proclaim God's Word may more effectively invite us to Eucharistic celebration. Each Eucharist is a precious opportunity for us to respond to our Father with hearts filled with awe and amazement at what he does for us through Jesus!

April 30, 1975   JEROME J. DuCHARME

CALENDAR OF MOVEABLE FEASTS AND SUNDAYS
(1975-1990)

Year	Sun-day Cy-cle	Week-day Cy-cle	Bapt. of Our Lord	First Sun. of Lent	East-er Sun-day	Pen-tecost Sun-day	Week of the Year	First Sun. Ad-vent
1975	A	I	Jan. 12	Feb. 16	Mar. 30	May 18	(VII)	Nov. 30
1976	B	II	Jan. 11	Mar. 7	Apr. 18	June 6	(X)	Nov. 28
1977	C	I	Jan. 9	Feb. 27	Apr. 10	May 29	(IX)	Nov. 27
1978	A	II	Jan. 8*	Feb. 12	Mar. 26	May 14	(VI)	Dec. 3
1979	B	I	Jan. 7*	Mar. 4	Apr. 15	June 3	(IX)	Dec. 2
1980	C	II	Jan. 13	Feb. 24	Apr. 6	May 25	(VIII)	Nov. 30
1981	A	I	Jan. 11	Mar. 8	Apr. 19	June 7	(X)	Nov. 29
1982	B	II	Jan. 10	Feb. 28	Apr. 11	May 30	(IX)	Nov. 28
1983	C	I	Jan. 9	Feb. 20	Apr. 3	May 22	(VIII)	Nov. 27
1984	A	II	Jan. 8*	Mar. 11	Apr. 22	June 10	(X)	Dec. 2
1985	B	I	Jan. 13	Feb. 24	Apr. 7	May 26	(VIII)	Dec. 1
1986	C	II	Jan. 12	Feb. 16	Mar. 30	May 18	(VII)	Nov. 30
1987	A	I	Jan. 11	Mar. 8	Apr. 19	June 7	(X)	Nov. 29
1988	B	II	Jan. 10	Feb. 21	Apr. 3	May 22	(VIII)	Nov. 27
1989	C	I	Jan. 8*	Feb. 12	Mar. 26	May 14	(VI)	Dec. 3
1990	A	II	Jan. 7*	Mar. 4	Apr. 15	June 3	(IX)	Dec. 2

*In the U. S., on this Sunday, the feast of the Epiphany of Our Lord is observed, and the feast of the Baptism of Our Lord is omitted. The week days following this Sunday are the First Week of the Year; and the Weeks of the Year follow consecutively until Ash Wednesday, the Wednesday before the first Sunday of Lent. The Weeks of the Year are resumed during the week following the feast of Pentecost, in such a way that the 34th Week of the Year is always the week before the First Sunday of Advent. The number of the Week of the Year in Pentecost Week is indicated by the Roman numeral after the date of Pentecost Sunday.

	Sun. after Bapt. of Our Lord	Sun. before Ash Wed.	Sundays of the Year	Sun. after Corpus Christi (U.S.)	Sun. before Christ King	Sundays of the Year
SUNDAYS OF THE YEAR FROM 1975 TO 1990						
Year						
1975	Jan. 19 - Feb. 9:		II - V	June 8 - Nov. 16:		X - XXXIII
1976	Jan. 18 - Feb. 29:		II - VIII	June 27 - Nov. 14:		XIII - XXXIII
1977	Jan. 16 - Feb. 20:		II - VII	June 19 - Nov. 13:		XII - XXXIII
1978	Jan. 15* - Feb. 5:		II - V	June 4 - Nov 19:		IX - XXXIII
1979	Jan. 14* - Feb. 25:		II - VIII	June 24 - Nov. 18:		XII - XXXIII
1980	Jan. 20 - Feb. 17:		II - VI	June 15 - Nov. 16:		XI - XXXIII
1981	Jan. 18 - Mar. 1:		II - VIII	June 28 - Nov. 15:		XIII - XXXIII
1982	Jan. 17 - Feb. 21:		II - VII	June 20 - Nov. 14:		XII - XXXIII
1983	Jan. 16 - Feb. 13:		II - VI	June 12 - Nov. 13:		XI - XXXIII
1984	Jan. 15* - Mar. 4:		II - IX	July 1 - Nov. 18:		XIII - XXXIII
1985	Jan. 20 - Feb. 17:		II - VI	June 16 - Nov. 17:		XI - XXXIII
1986	Jan. 19 - Feb. 9:		II - V	June 8 - Nov. 16:		X - XXXIII
1987	Jan. 18 - Mar. 1:		II - VIII	June 28 - Nov. 15:		XIII - XXXIII
1988	Jan. 17 - Feb. 14:		II - VI	June 12 - Nov. 13:		XI - XXXIII
1989	Jan. 15* - Feb. 5:		II - V	June 4 - Nov. 19:		IX - XXXIII
1990	Jan. 14* - Feb. 25:		II - VIII	June 24 - Nov. 18:		XII - XXXIII

*Sunday after Epiphany in the U.S.

CONTENTS

HOLY WEEK

EASTER SEASON

SUNDAYS IN ORDINARY TIME

OTHER MAJOR FEASTS

ABBREVIATIONS

Old Testament

Gn	Genesis	Prv	Proverbs
Ex	Exodus	Wis	Wisdom
Lv	Leviticus	Sir	Sirach
Nm	Numbers	Is	Isaiah
Dt	Deuteronomy	Jer	Jeremiah
Jos	Joshua	Bar	Baruch
1 Sm	1 Samuel	Ez	Ezechiel
2 Sm	2 Samuel	Dn	Daniel
1 Kgs	1 Kings	Hos	Hosea
2 Kgs	2 Kings	Am	Amos
2 Chr	2 Chronicles	Jon	Jonah
Jb	Job	Mal	Malachi

New Testament

Mt	Matthew	Col	Colossians
Mk	Mark	1 Thes	1 Thessalonians
Lk	Luke	2 Tm	2 Timothy
Jn	John	Ti	Titus
Acts	Acts of the	Heb	Hebrews
	Apostles	Jas	James
Rom	Romans	1 Pt	1 Peter
1 Cor	1 Corinthians	2 Pt	2 Peter
2 Cor	2 Corinthians	1 Jn	1 John
Gal	Galatians	Rv	Revelation
Eph	Ephesians		(Apocalypse)
Phil	Philippians		

ADVENT SEASON

I SUNDAY
OF ADVENT

Is 63:16–17,19; 64:2–7
1 Cor 1:3–9
Mk 13:33–37

The first three Sundays in the Cycle "B" Advent Season give us the opportunity to renew the commitment we first made on the day of our baptism.

Today's second reading reminds us of how God called us at baptism to "die" to our sinful ways (Rom 6:2–7) and to "rise" to new life and fellowship with Jesus (1 Cor 1:9; Rom 6:8). At our baptism we began to share in the risen life of our Lord. In today's Eucharistic celebration, we express our belief and expectation that God will completely reveal his saving work in us at the final coming of Jesus, "the day of our Lord Jesus Christ" (1 Cor 1:8).

In the powerful first reading, the prophet Isaiah speaks on behalf of the Israelites and admits that they have forgotten God. No longer do they even attempt to center their lives around the God of the Sinai convenant. The Israelites sin because of their failure to respond to God's love for them (Is 63:17,19). Isaiah recognizes that salvation is a gift from God and that only God can change the hearts of the people. The prophet humbly admits the people's need for God and confidently begs God to save them: "No ear has ever heard, no eye has ever seen, any God but you doing such deeds for those who wait for him" (Is 64:3).

In his first letter to the Christians at Corinth, Paul encourages them to hope in God for their salvation: "That you lack no spiritual gift as you wait for the revelation of our Lord Jesus Christ. He will strengthen you to the end" (1 Cor 1:7,8). In this reading Paul tells us that God will not abandon us when we genuinely trust in him: "God is faithful, and it was he who called you to fellowship with his Son, Jesus Christ our Lord" (1 Cor 1:9).

In the gospel, Jesus warns us to prepare now for his final coming: "Be constantly on the watch! Stay awake!" (Mk 13:33) "Be on guard!" (Mk 13:37)

In today's Eucharistic liturgy, we respond with love to our Father who has called us "to fellowship with his Son, Jesus Christ our Lord" (1 Cor 1:9). Heeding Jesus' gospel warning to "look around you" (Mk 13:35), we realize that God's saving work continues in us through Jesus present among us today. Here and now he is freeing us from our sins and transforming us with his risen life. In our Eucharistic prayer, we express our willingness to be saved by Jesus, as we await the full effects of our salvation on the last day, "the revelation of our Lord Jesus Christ" (1 Cor 1:7).

II SUNDAY OF ADVENT

Is 40:1–5, 9–11
2 Pt 3:8–14
Mk 1:1–8

Today we proclaim the Good News of salvation to our brothers and sisters. Our salvation, which is a sharing in the risen life of Jesus, began for us in baptism. Now we eagerly await "the day of the Lord" (2 Pt 3:10), that day when we will experience fully our life in Jesus.

In the first reading, Isaiah announces a message of hope to the troubled people of Israel: "Comfort, give comfort to my people, says your God" (Is 40:1). Isaiah enthusiastically proclaims the awesome coming of God, who will bring salvation to the people: "Here is your God! Here comes in power the Lord God" (Is 40:9,10).

The baptism preached by John the Baptist in today's gospel is not the same as our sacrament of baptism. Quoting from today's passage from Isaiah (Mk 1:2,3; Is 40:3), John invites the people to a profound religious conversion. He asks them to turn their minds and hearts to the God of Sinai. John is intense in his efforts to reach the people because God is about to offer his people his full gift of salvation in the person of Jesus: "One more powerful than I is to come after me. . . . he will baptize you in the Holy Spirit" (Mk 1:7,8).

Peter is writing to a community of early Christians. They have already opened their hearts to the Good News of salvation in Jesus and have accepted baptism. But the community was now experiencing a restlessness, expecting a quick coming of "the day of the Lord" (2 Pt 3:10). Peter encourages them to be patient as they await our Lord's final coming (2 Pt 3:9).

Today as we proclaim the Good News of salvation in Jesus, God calls all of us to open our hearts to Jesus. Our Father asks us to accept, with patience and trust, what at times seems to us to be a very slow growth in the life of Jesus. We respond to God by expressing our determination to live without sin, to grow in grace and to be at peace with one another (2 Pt 3:14,18). Joyfully we get ready to greet our risen Lord, who comes among us as we celebrate the Eucharist today: "Here is your God! Here comes with power the Lord God" (Is 40:9,10).

III SUNDAY OF ADVENT

Is 61:1,2, 10,11
1 Thes 5:16–24
Jn 1:6–8, 19–28

The theme of today's liturgy centers around our faith experience of the Spirit of Jesus. The three readings draw our attention to Jesus as the Spirit-filled Messiah. The risen Jesus, who first sent his Spirit into our hearts in baptism, is present among us as we celebrate today's Eucharist. Once again he sends the Spirit to us so that we can taste the peace and gladness which only the Spirit can give us.

In the first reading, Isaiah is elated as he joyfully proclaims that God has given him an experience of the Holy Spirit (Is 61:1). Isaiah then announces that God will bring complete joy and happiness into the world (Is 61:1–11; *also see* Is 11:1–9). This Old Testament prophecy is fulfilled in the risen Jesus, who sends the Spirit of God upon us.

We received the Spirit of Jesus for the first time in baptism. But to grow in the life of the Spirit, we must remain open to him: "Do not stifle the Spirit" (1 Thes 5:19). Since we cannot count on our own strength to guarantee our continued openness to the Spirit, we have to trust in God who promises to complete his saving work in us (1 Thes 5:23).

The gospel reading describes how John the Baptist faithfully performed his task of announcing the arrival of the Messiah. John was sent by God "only to testify to the light, for he himself was not the light" (Jn 1:8). This text is a reminder to us that our task as readers is always to call people's attention to Jesus.

The Jesus whom we proclaim today is present among us. Our risen Lord sends his Spirit into our hearts and invites us to experience a spirited, joyfilled Eucharist: "Rejoice always, never cease praying, render constant thanks; such is God's will for you in Christ Jesus" (1 Thes 5:16–18).

IV SUNDAY OF ADVENT

2 Sm 7:1–5, 8–11, 16
Rom 16:25–27
Lk 1:26–38

The Mass for the Fourth Sunday of Advent prepares us for the feast of Christmas, the birthday of our Lord. In today's three readings, we announce this Good News: Jesus, who is Mary's Son and David's descendant, is the fulfillment of all Old Testament prophecies.

In the first reading, King David expresses his intention to build a temple for God in order to house the ark in an appropriate manner (2 Sm 7:1,2). This was a sign of David's devotion because the ark symbolized God's continuing presence among his people. Nathan, God's spokesman, replies to the King with the surprising news that it is God, not David, who will do the building. God promises to build a lasting dynasty for David: "Your

house and your kingdom shall endure forever before me"
(2 Sm 7:16). Nathan's prophecy helps us to understand
better the Jesus whom we proclaim today to our brothers
and sisters in the words of Paul: "I preach Jesus Christ,
the gospel [the Good News] which reveals the mystery
hidden for many ages, but now manifested through the
writings of the prophets" (Rom 16:25,26).

Today's gospel reading tells us the Good News that
Nathan's prophecy has been fulfilled in Jesus. Our Lord
was born "to a virgin betrothed to a man named Joseph,
of the house of David. . . . The Lord God will give him
the throne of David his father. He will rule over the
house of Jacob forever and his reign will be without end"
(Lk 1:27,32,33).

The Jesus whom we proclaim in the readings is not
a person who is "buried" in past history. Our risen Savior
is alive and in our midst as we celebrate today's Eucharist.
Aware of our Lord's continuing presence among us, we
give praise to our heavenly Father: "To him, the God
who alone is wise, may glory be given through Jesus
Christ unto endless ages. Amen!" (Rom 16:27)

CHRISTMAS AND EPIPHANY

December 25
CHRISTMAS
Mass at Midnight

Is 9:1–6
Ti 2:11–14
Lk 2:1–14

On this special night of the year, we consider the mystery of God's love for us: "The grace of God has appeared, offering salvation to all men" (Ti 2:11). Our salvation is not the result of our own efforts. We are saved because of God's loving initiative in sending us Jesus. It is now our choice, freely and lovingly, to respond to our Father by accepting Jesus as our Savior.

In all three readings, we proclaim the theme of God's initiative of love toward us. Isaiah tells us: "The people who walked in darkness have seen a great light" (Is 9:1). "For a child is born to us, a son is given us" (Is 9:5). God's love for us is described even in military terms as Isaiah reminds the people of the Old Testament of the battle in which God rescued them from the hands of the Midianites (Is 9:3,4; Judges, chapters 6-8).

Paul writes to Titus: "The grace of God has appeared, offering salvation to all men" (Ti 2:11). In the Bible, the "grace of God" means the sum total of all God's gifts to us, in particular, the Father's gift of his Son to be our Savior.

In Luke's gospel, the angels praise God in song for his love for mankind: "Glory to God in high heaven, peace on earth to those on whom his favor rests" (Lk 2:14).

Our Father sends us his Son in tonight's Eucharistic celebration. God reaffirms his permanent commitment of love toward us and toward all men. Jesus our brother, the greatest gift our Father could ever give us, is present among us as we gather together to celebrate the Father's love for us. Jesus becomes present in his act of self-sacrifice, by which he cleanses us and transforms us into God's own people, "eager to do what is right" (Ti 2:14).

Proclaim the Good News: We who do not deserve

God's mercy have become God's very own people. In Jesus we are reconciled to our Father.

December 25
CHRISTMAS
Mass at Dawn

Is 62:11–12
Ti 3:4–7
Lk 2:15–20

Today, all over the world, readers proclaim the Good News of the birth of Jesus. As we proclaim this exciting message, God speaks to his people through us: "See, the LORD proclaims to the ends of the earth: Say to the daughter of Zion, your savior comes!" (Is 62:11).

Through Jesus, we have become God's holy people (Is 62:12). Paul, in his letter to his friend, Titus, reminds us that Jesus saved us not because of any righteousness on our part. We are saved because of the mercy God shows toward us in Jesus (Ti 3:4,5).

As we celebrate the Eucharist today, we are aware that Jesus is our Immanuel (God with us). We pray with longing for our full inheritance, our complete salvation in Jesus: "That we might be justified by his grace and become heirs, in hope, of eternal life" (Ti 3:7).

December 25
CHRISTMAS
Mass during the Day

Is 52:7–10
Heb 1:1–6
Jn 1:1–18 (Long Form),
or Jn 1:1–5, 9–14 (Short Form)

Today, the birthday of our Savior, we announce the Good News: God has sent his Son who reveals the Father to us. Since it is our role as readers to make such an exciting announcement, the first verses of the passage from Isaiah can be applied to ourselves: "How beautiful upon the mountains are the feet of him who brings glad tidings, announcing peace, bearing good news, announcing salvation, and saying to Zion, 'Your God is King!'" (Is 52:7).

What we proclaim in the first reading is actually happening to our worshipping community today: The Lord is restoring, comforting and redeeming us in Jesus (Is 52:8,9). "All the ends of the earth will behold the salvation of our God" (Is 52:10).

In the second and third readings, we are challenged to ask ourselves the question: Who is Jesus? Jesus is he who comes forth from the Father. He is the fulness of what the Father wishes to say to us. Jesus not only delivers God's complete message. He is personally God's Word, in whom the Father expresses himself to us and to the world: "In the times past, God spoke in fragmentary and varied ways to our fathers through the prophets; in this, the final age, he has spoken to us through his Son. . . . This Son is the reflection of the Father's glory, the exact representation of the Father's being" (Heb 1:1,2,3).

The gospel text describes Jesus as the Light which continues to shine in the darkness (Jn 1:5). He is filled with life which he shares with those who accept him (Jn 1:12). "The Word became flesh and made his dwelling among us" (Jn 1:14). The gospel reading (Long Form) ends with two powerful statements which point out, once again, Jesus' role as revealer of the Father: "No one has ever seen God. It is God the only Son, ever at the Father's side, who has revealed him" (Jn 1:18).

God speaks to the people today as we proclaim the Scripture readings. As God speaks, he also strengthens the faith of our community so that we are better able to experience Jesus in the Eucharistic Liturgy. God's Word, Jesus, is alive among us: "We have seen his glory: The glory of an only Son coming from the Father, filled with enduring love" (Jn 1:14). In his first letter, John describes his awareness in faith that Jesus is alive in our midst: "This is what we proclaim to you: what was from the beginning, what we have heard, what we have seen

with our eyes . . . and our hands have touched—we speak
of the word of life. . . . we proclaim to you the eternal
life that was present to the Father and became visible to
us" (I Jn 1:1,2) .

Sunday in the Octave of Christmas HOLY FAMILY

Sir 3:2–6, 12–14
Col 3:12–21
Lk 2:22–40 (Long Form),
or Lk 2:22, 39,40 (Short Form)

Today's readings center around family life and the
relationships we have within our families. There are two
families to be considered: our family at home and our
larger family, the community with which we worship
each Sunday.

Through baptism, we have become brothers and
sisters in Jesus. But this does not mean that our family at
home is on the natural level, while our larger family is
supernatural. The smaller family can be appropriately
regarded as a "little church" because it is the smallest
unit for love relationships within the larger christian
community. Our family at home, including our spouse,
children, parents, brothers and sisters, is a christian community in miniature.

The four gospels tell us very little about the family
life of Jesus, Mary and Joseph. Even today's gospel high-
lights Simeon and Anna, who represent the faithful people
of Israel. The Holy Spirit inspires both of them to recognize Jesus as the long-awaited Messiah. They rejoice in
the Spirit and give praise to God (Lk 2:25–32) .

The reading from Sirach is in the style of Old Testament wisdom literature. The passage gives some prover-
bial admonitions about family life. In this text, Sirach
speaks only of the relationship of children toward their
parents. The very same attitude of filial respect is repeated in a parallel manner in each verse of the reading.

In the second reading, St. Paul first speaks to the

larger family, the christian community at Colossus. They
are God's chosen ones, holy and affectionately loved by
God (Col 3:12). Since the Colossians are so loved by
God, Paul admonishes them to "Bear with one another.
. . . forgive as the Lord has forgiven you. Over all these
virtues put on love, which binds the rest together and
makes them perfect" (Col. 3:13,14). Paul then speaks
to the family at home . He urges the Colossians to develop
stronger family relations (Col 3:18-21). Paul's advice
is not a mere list of "do's and don'ts." He is challenging
the early Christians to have an open, loving attitude toward
each other.

The risen Jesus is completely loving and open toward
us and toward all people. As risen Lord, he is the source
of the openness that we strive for in our human relationships. Jesus is especially the source of our efforts to heal
the hurt and pain we so often inflict on those we love.

We are challenged today to be more aware of Jesus,
present among us in our worshipping community and in
our homes. His gift to us is the warmth and closeness
that we all need to grow as persons. To receive Jesus' gift,
we must be willing to act in the spirit of his openness:
"Whatever you do, whether in speech or in action, do
in the name of the Lord Jesus. Give thanks to God the
Father through him" (Col 3:17).

January 1—Octave of Christmas
SOLEMNITY OF MARY,
MOTHER OF GOD

Nm 6:22-27
Gal 4:4-7
Lk 2:16-21

Christian prayer is the theme of today's Liturgy of
the Word. The readings challenge us to appreciate and
deepen our prayer experience.

Aaron and his sons are the priestly family among the
Israelites. In the reading from Numbers, God gives Aaron
and his sons a special commission. They are to pray by

invoking God's name on behalf of the people: "So shall
they invoke my name upon the Israelites, and I will bless
them" (Nm 6:27).

In the Old Testament, the invoking of God's name
went beyond an ordinary prayer of petition. The Israelites
approached God in prayer with a deep sense of being
part of the chosen people. Throughout the Old Testament, God describes his covenant relationship with the
Israelites in a simple but beautiful way: "You shall be
my people, and I will be your God" (Ez 36:28). As the
Israelites prayed, they were keenly aware of belonging to
the people whom God favored when he initiated the
covenant with Moses at Sinai.

Prayer is one of the main themes in Luke's gospel.
In today's passage, the shepherds' visit raises questions
in Mary's mind: Who is this child who will save the people? How will he accomplish his mission? Mary's attitude
is calm and prayerful as she "treasured all these things
and reflected on them in her heart" (Lk 2:19).

In his letter to the Galatians, Paul speaks of that
time when God began his new and lasting covenant with
us: "When the designated time had come, God sent forth
his Son born of a woman. . . . so that we might receive
our status as adopted sons" (Gal 4:4,5). In baptism, God
has become our Father. We are brothers and sisters in
Jesus. We have so often heard that God is our Father
that we take this privilege for granted. Our challenge
today is to deepen our appreciation of what it means to
stand before God as his sons and daughters.

Since we are alive in the risen Jesus, we are called
to share also in Jesus' prayer experience. Jesus, our
brother, is prayerfully aware that his life is a continuing
gift from his Father. The proof that we are adopted sons
of God is not a legal certificate. As Paul tells us, "the
proof that you are sons is that God has sent forth into our
hearts the spirit of his Son which cries out 'Abba!'
('Father!')" (Gal 4:6).

Our Father sends Jesus, our brother, to be among us
today as we celebrate the Eucharist. The Mass is our

special time to renew our covenant relationship with God: "I will be your Father, and you shall be my people, alive in my Son!" Our worship becomes a more meaningful prayer as we become more conscious of what it means to be alive in Jesus, with God as our Father.

Early in the Second Century, Ignatius of Antioch described our Father's mysterious call to us which invites us to respond to him in the Eucharist: "There is living water in me, which speaks and says inside me, 'Come to the Father'" (Ignatius' Letter to the Romans, 7:2). We celebrate the Eucharist today as a people spirited in Jesus, crying out "Abba, Father!" (Gal 4:6).

Second Sunday after CHRISTMAS

Sir 24:1–4, 8–12
Eph 1:3–6, 15–18
Jn 1:1–18 (Long Form)
or Jn 1:1–5, 9–14

Today's first reading, from the Book of Sirach, is about wisdom. Among the people of ancient times, wisdom was a kind of humanism. It was based on a spiritual reflection which led people to become more prudent in their ways, so that they could lead successful lives. The quest for wisdom was common to all cultures in the ancient world. Israel's search for wisdom had certain similarities to other cultures, but there was one major difference. Israel recognized that her wisdom originated from Yahweh, her God. It was the Israelites' task to discover God's wisdom and to fashion their lifestyle accordingly.

Sirach poetically personifies Wisdom. Wisdom sings her own praises: "From the mouth of the Most High I came forth" (Sir 24:3). Wisdom is created by God and lives with God from the beginning (Sir 24:9). Wisdom also makes her dwelling place among the people: "He who formed me chose the spot for my tent, saying, 'In Jacob make your dwelling, in Israel your inheritance'" (Sir 24:8).

In John's Prologue, today's third reading, there are

parallels to the reading from Sirach. In John, however,
God's wisdom is definitely a person, the person of God's
eternal Son. The Word who existed with God from the
very beginning "became flesh and made his dwelling
among us" (Jn 1:14).

The second reading is from Paul's letter to the Christians at Ephesus. In the Incarnation, Paul writes, the
mysterious plan conceived by God from all eternity is
fulfilled. It is impossible for us to understand God's plan
unless we are blessed with God's own special wisdom and
enlightenment: "God has given us the wisdom to understand fully the mystery, the plan he was pleased to decree
in Christ" (Eph 1:9,10). What is God's plan? "God
chose us in him (Jesus) before the world began, to be
holy and blameless in his sight, to be full of love; he likewise predestined us through Christ Jesus to be adopted
sons—such was his will and pleasure—that all might praise
the glorious favor he has bestowed on us in his beloved"
(Eph 1:4–6). From all eternity we have been in the mind
and heart of our Father. The ultimate objective in God's
plan is to make us his adopted sons and daughters in Jesus.

As we come to a deeper realization of how we are
personally involved in God's eternal plan in Jesus, our
most appropriate response is loving praise and gratitude:
"Praised be the God and Father of our Lord Jesus Christ,
who has bestowed on us in Christ every spiritual blessing
in the heavens!" (Eph 1:3) In the Eucharist, we say "thank
you" to our Father in a manner most pleasing to him.
We thank him through Jesus, his Son.

January 6
EPIPHANY

Is 60:1,6
Eph 3:2,3, 5,6
Mt 2:1:12

Every year, we celebrate in the liturgy three events
in the life of Jesus in which he manifested that he was
both God's Son and the promised Messiah. Each mani-

festation of the Lord points toward his dying and rising, the fulfillment of all messianic prophecies. The three manifestations (epiphanies) are: (1) Today's feast, the manifestation of the Christ Child to the Magi; (2) The Baptism of Jesus, usually celebrated on the Sunday after the Epiphany; (3) The Transfiguration, commemorated both on the Second Sunday of Lent and on August 6th.

The revelation of the identity of Jesus is made only to believers, to people who accept their faith experience as a gift from God. When we celebrate the Lord's self-manifestations, we are in fact celebrating our gift of faith. In today's three readings, faith is described as a gift which God bestows on Jews and Gentiles alike.

The Magi are not Jews. They are "outsiders" from the East. They follow the star and when they discover Jesus, the Messiah, they believe in him (Mt 2:1-12).

In the second reading, Paul also speaks of the universality of God's gift of faith: "In Christ Jesus the Gentiles are now co-heirs with the Jews, members of the same body and sharers of the promise made through the preaching of the gospel" (Eph 3:6).

The Old Testament times were certainly privileged years for the Jews: "Rise up in splendor, Jerusalem! Your light has come, the glory of the Lord shines upon you" (Is 60:1). Isaiah goes on to say that God's self-revelation in Jerusalem will be not only for the Jews, but for all people (Is 60:2-6). God generously invites all people to believe in his Son.

Today, our Father calls us together to experience the Eucharist as a believing community. We share the same fellowship of faith as "members of the same body" (Eph 3:6). If we are willing to accept each person in our worshipping community, then we will come to a deeper realization of what it means to be part of a community of believers. Our faith is a gift we share with others. We are all seeking Jesus, our Light, who is present among us as we celebrate the Eucharist.

Sunday after January 6
BAPTISM OF THE LORD

Is 42:1–4, 6,7
Acts 10:34–38
Mk 1:6–11

The Baptism of Jesus is the second manifestation of his messianic mission. He is again identified as God's Chosen One and our human brother.

The first reading gives some Old Testament background for the gospel narrative of Jesus' Baptism. God describes the Messiah: "Here is my servant whom I uphold, my chosen one with whom I am pleased, upon whom I have put my spirit" (Is 42:1). God then speaks to the Servant: "I formed you, and set you as a covenant of the people, a light for the nations" (Is 42:6).

In Acts, Paul accepts into the community of believers the Gentile Cornelius and his family. The Good News which they believe in is "what has been reported all over Judea about Jesus of Nazareth, beginning in Galilee with the baptism John preached; of the way God anointed him (Jesus) with the Holy Spirit and power" (Acts 10:37,38).

Jesus did not ask to receive baptism because he was a sinner. He wanted to be baptized in order to manifest his true identity and mission: he was sent by his Father to be one of us so that he would save us. Jesus lovingly accepts the task his Father gives him. He decides to save us through his suffering, dying, and rising. In being baptized, Jesus expressed his "yes" to his Father, the "yes" which would be more perfectly realized in his dying. In the gospel, the Father shows his love and acceptance of Jesus: "Immediately on coming up out of the water he saw the sky rent in two and the Spirit descending on him like a dove. Then a voice came from the heavens: 'You are my beloved Son. On you my favor rests' " (Mk 1:10, 11). The Father will most completely express his acceptance of Jesus when he will raise Jesus from the dead.

As we celebrate the Eucharist, we are asked to manifest our own identity as the people of the new covenant. Our risen Messiah is here with us to help us as we gather to worship. Jesus is fully the delight of his Father. He is now overflowing with the Spirit as he continues to express his total and complete "yes" to his Father. Jesus is the only way that we can successfully approach our Father. Today in offering ourselves with Jesus to the Father, we are saying: "Here is your beloved Son. Your favor rests on him" (*See* Mk 1:11).

LENTEN SEASON

FIRST SUNDAY
OF LENT

Gn 9:8–15
1 Pt 3:18–22
Mk 1:12–15

The readings for the first five Sundays in Lent have been carefully selected to prepare us for Holy Week and our celebration of Jesus' death and Resurrection. This Sunday's readings call our attention to the covenant which God has made with us in Jesus.

God's Son became one of us to give us sinners the awesome privilege of relating to his Father as our Father: "This is why Christ died . . . that he might lead you to God" (1 Pt 3:18; see Jn 20:17). In our Eucharistic meal today, we renew our covenant with God, our love relationship with the Father of Jesus.

According to the Bible, every profound love relationship between God and mankind is called a covenant. God initiates each covenant by expressing his love for people in a most moving manner. (For instance, God favored Noah and his family and saved them from the flood.) God then invites his beloved people to return his love. The covenant which God made with Noah is the first such relationship mentioned in Genesis, after the sin of Adam and Eve.

The most important covenant in the Old Testament was the Sinai covenant. Before Jesus came, God kept urging his chosen people to be faithful to this covenant. But the Israelites never fully appreciated the extent of God's love for them, and their response never measured up to God's expectations. Finally, in Jesus, God's love for his people found its full response. In Jesus our Brother, God has made his definitive and lasting covenant with us and with all mankind.

Because of his unique relationship with his heavenly Father, Jesus was continually aware of the full extent of his Father's love for him. In return for his Father's generous love, Jesus lovingly accepted whatever his Father sent him. In today's gospel, Jesus is tempted (Mk 1:12,13), but he refuses to waver from his commitment of love toward his Father. Later, Jesus would completely express his love for his Father in his love-filled death on the cross.

In the second reading, Peter sees a parallel between God's covenant with Noah and our baptism. We approached the waters of baptism and accepted God's saving love for us as manifested in Jesus' death and Resurrection. Peter tells us that we "are now saved by a baptismal bath" (1 Pt 3:21). Our risen Brother, by sharing his life with us, brings us through the waters of baptism to a new relationship with his Father (*See* Rom 6:3–11). Alive in our risen Savior, we can now be faithful to our Father and successfully live in covenant relationship with him.

In the gospel reading, our Father invites us to open our hearts to Jesus, his gift of love to us: "This is the time of fulfillment! The reign of God is at hand! Reform your lives and believe in the Good News!" (Mk 1:15). Our Father truly makes an overture of love toward us today by sending his risen Son to be among us as we celebrate our Eucharist. In the Eucharist, our covenant meal, we renew our love relationship with our Father. Eagerly we recommit ourselves to be his faithful sons and daughters, alive in Jesus!

SECOND SUNDAY OF LENT

Gn 22:1,2, 9, 10–13, 15–18
Rom 8:31–34
Mk 9:2–10

The theme of today's Liturgy of the Word challenges us to deepen our faith in Jesus, our risen Savior. We have the opportunity today to express our belief: The same Jesus, who died and was raised by the Father (Rom 8:34), continues his active presence among us in our Eucharistic celebration.

In the reading from Genesis, God puts Abraham "to the test" (Gn 22:1). God asks Abraham to perform a most difficult task—to sacrifice Isaac, his only son, his beloved.

It is inspiring to see how Abraham responds so eagerly and wholeheartedly: "Ready!" (Gn 22:1) "Yes, Lord!" (Gn 22:11) Because of Abraham's exceptional faith and obedience, he is called the "father of all believers" (Gal 3:6–9). What a challenge it is for us to become like Abraham in our response to God: "Yes, Lord!" (Gn 22:11) But we cannot allow ourselves to be satisfied with merely imitating Abraham's faith. He believed in God's promise of salvation. We are privileged to believe in Jesus, the fulfilment of that promise.

In the second reading, we proclaim a strong message of hope: "If God is for us, who can be against us?" (Rom 8:31) God has demonstrated, once and for all, his total and lasting commitment of love toward us by sending his Son to die for us: God "did not spare his own Son" (Rom 8:32). God's saving love is fully revealed to us in the dying and rising of Jesus.

The third reading is Mark's account of Jesus' Transfiguration. Peter, James and John were "overcome with awe" (Mk 9:6) as they witnessed this unique preview of our Lord's Resurrection. Mark mentions how Jesus cautioned the three men: "He strictly enjoined them not to tell anyone what they had seen, before the Son of Man had risen from the dead" (Mk 9:9). We can now see in this restriction a disguised invitation to us as readers that we enthusiastically proclaim the Good News of the risen Jesus to our brothers and sisters.

Our risen Lord is present among us as we celebrate today's Eucharist. He is the same Jesus who was once transfigured before Peter, James and John. Our Father invites us today to stake our very lives on Jesus: "This is my Son, my beloved. Listen to him" (Mk 9:7). By opening our hearts to Jesus, the Father's beloved in our midst, and by listening to him, we express our complete trust in our heavenly Father: "If God is for us, who can be against us? . . . Who shall bring a charge against God's chosen ones?" (Rom 8:31, 33)

THIRD SUNDAY
OF LENT

Ex 20:1–17 (Long Form),
or Ex 20:1–3, 7,8, 12–17 (Short Form)
1 Cor 1:22–25
Jn 2:13–25

The readings for the Third Sunday of Lent are set in the context of God's two tremendous saving acts in salvation history: the deliverance of the Jews from Egyptian slavery, and God's deliverance of his new people, ourselves, from sin through Jesus' death and Resurrection. Because God tells us in the readings how much he loves us in Jesus, we are challenged to respond to our Father with love in our Eucharistic celebration.

In the Scripture reading from Exodus, God insists that the Israelites pattern their lifestyle according to the commandments. God gave the commandments in the context of the mutual love relationship of the Sinai covenant. Instead of being merely an arbitrary list of regulations, the commandments are described as the chosen people's loving response to God: "I, the Lord, am your God, who brought you out of the land of Egypt, that place of slavery" (Ex 22:2).

Like the first reading, the gospel is also set in the context of Israel's Sinai experience: "The Jewish Passover was near" (Jn 2:13). The gospel centers around the temple, which was built to be the privileged place for Jewish worship (*See* 2 Chr 5:1–10). Faithful Jews made pilgrimages to the temple for certain holydays, especially Passover, in order to recall vividly how God loved them and made them his very own people. Prescribed Jewish rituals helped God's people recommit themselves to the Sinai covenant.

When Jesus entered the temple area that day, he knew that merchants were needed to sell what was necessary for the rituals. But Jesus became angry because he saw how monetary transactions were being emphasized, rather than loving response to God. After Jesus displays his indignation, he makes a very mysterious announcement: "Destroy this temple. . . . and in three days I will raise it up" (Jn 2:19). Jesus claims to be God's new temple. The followers of Jesus are baffled to hear Jesus refer to himself as a temple. "Only after Jesus had been raised from the dead did his disciples recall that he had said this" (Jn 2:22). In dying, Jesus, God's living temple, would express the most perfect and complete human response to God's love.

After our Lord's Resurrection, his followers became aware of the new way in which Jesus was present among them. We too are growing in our awareness that the risen Jesus is still with us and sends his Spirit into our hearts as we celebrate the Eucharist. The Spirit of Jesus moves us to accept God's "foolishness," Jesus crucified (1 Cor 1:22–25), who has become our life-giving Savior.

Because our risen Lord is with us today, we can respond to our Father in a manner which pleases him—in the Spirit of Jesus: "An hour is coming, and is already here, when authentic worshippers will worship the Father in Spirit and truth. Indeed, it is just such worshippers the Father seeks" (Jn 4:23).

FOURTH SUNDAY OF LENT

2 Ch 36:14–16, 19–23
Eph 2:4–10
Jn 3:14–21

Today we proclaim Jesus Christ, our Father's gift of salvation to us! We express our gratitude to our Father in our Eucharistic celebration. We also reaffirm in our worship our decision to accept Jesus as our Savior and to live as our Father's faithful people.

The first reading describes God's unfailing love for Israel. The God of Sinai sends prophet after prophet to his people to remind them of his love for them (2 Chr 36:15). But the Israelites are coldhearted and unresponsive "until the anger of the Lord against his people was so inflamed that there was no remedy" (2 Chr 36:16). The invading Chaldeans kill many Israelites, burn their temple and send the survivors into exile. Nevertheless, God does not abandon his people. Through Cyrus, King of Persia, God rescues his undeserving people and returns them to their homeland. In the Bible, man's salvation is always regarded as a complete gift from God.

In no way did the Israelites deserve God's favor. In no way do we deserve God's complete gift of salvation in Jesus. "It is owing to his favor that salvation is yours through faith. This is not your doing, it is God's gift" (Eph 2:8). Our Father has sent his Son to die for us and to be raised, "lifted up" (Jn 3:14), so that "whoever believes in him may not die but may have eternal life" (Jn 3:16).

Jesus is God's final and most perfect gift to us. We acknowledge our love and gratitude to our Father by celebrating the Eucharist with our minds and hearts focused on our risen Lord, present among us. Because we are a people who are now alive in Jesus, we are able to please our heavenly Father in our prayers and in our actions (Eph 2:10; Jn 3:19-21). Through Jesus, we are acceptable to the Father: "No one comes to the Father but through me" (Jn 14:6).

FIFTH SUNDAY OF LENT

Jer 31:31–34
Heb 5:7–9
Jn 12:20–33

Today's theme, God's covenant with us in Jesus, closely coincides with the theme we celebrated four weeks ago on the First Sunday of Lent. With Holy Week just seven days away, the Church wisely insists that we once again give serious, prayerful consideration to our relationship with God.

Do we ever allow ourselves to be surprised by God's love for us? Throughout salvation history, God has manifested his love for mankind in many ways. "In this, the final age, he has spoken to us through his Son" (Heb

1:2). In today's readings, God invites us to be moved by the love he shows us in the death and Resurrection of Jesus.

Speaking through Jeremiah, God promises the Israelites a new, lasting covenant: "It will not be like the covenant I made with their fathers . . . for they broke my covenant" (Jer 31:32). God reveals his new and eternal love relationship with us in the events of Jesus' life, particularly in his dying and rising. By sending Jesus to us, God demonstrates that his covenant with us will last forever. Jesus is our Father's complete and irrevocable gift of himself to us: "Jesus Christ . . . was not alternately 'yes' and 'no'; he was never anything but 'yes.' Whatever promises God has made have been fulfilled in him" (2 Cor 1:19,20).

In Jesus we also find the most complete and perfect response to God's love. By dying for us, Jesus gave himself totally to his Father: "What shall I say—Father, save me from this hour? But it was for this that I came to this hour" (Jn 12:27).

The new and lasting covenant flows from the love relationship between Jesus and his Father as manifested in the New Testament writings. In order for us to become actively involved in Jesus' covenant with his Father, we have to believe in Jesus as our Savior and be reborn in his Spirit: "When perfected, he [Jesus] became the source of eternal salvation for all who obey him" (Heb 5:9). By dying and rising, Jesus has won for us the opportunity to share in his risen life. Sharing in the life of Jesus means that we are able to share in his mysterious experience of relating to God as his Father. Through Jesus, we have truly become God's adopted sons and daughters: "See what love the Father has bestowed on us in letting us be called children of God! Yet that is what we are . . . we are God's children now" (1 Jn 3:1, 2).

How often have we heard that God loves us completely in Jesus? We miss out on so much in our love affair with God when we are worried about what we "must do" as Christians. Only when we "let go" and allow ourselves to be surprised by God's love for us can we begin to respond to our Father with greater spontaneity and generosity.

Our risen Brother is with us today: "See what love the Father has bestowed on us!" (1 Jn 3:1) Through Jesus and with Jesus, we gratefully celebrate our love relationship with our Father in today's Eucharist, our covenant meal.

HOLY WEEK

Passion Sunday
PALM SUNDAY

Is 50:4–7
Phil 2:6–11
Mk 14:1 – 15:47 (Long Form),
or Mk 15:1–39 (Short Form)

Holy Week is more than a mere recalling of the final events in the life of Jesus. During these special days, we strive for a better insight into how the Easter mystery of Jesus (his suffering, dying and rising) is our mystery too. We are not onlookers or outsiders to the events of Holy Week. The Spirit of the risen Jesus lives in us, his people, and transforms us from within so that in a life-long effort, we may become more Christlike (Son-like) in the way we think and love: "Your attitude must be that of Christ" (Phil 2:6).

In the first reading, Isaiah reports the words of the mysterious Suffering Servant of Yahweh. The Servant, whose mission is to save the people, is subjected to many unjust trials and afflictions. Because the Servant remains faithful to God and trusts so completely in him, God does not fail him.

For us readers, the second reading (Phil 2:6–11) is certainly one of our greatest challenges to excellent procla-mation. In this short passage, Paul summarizes in a hymn of praise the entire life, death, and resurrection of Jesus. An unhurried verse by verse reflection is our best way to prepare for this proclamation. Jesus, God's eternal Son, became one of us in a very unpretentious way: not as risen Lord in glory, but as humble Servant (Phil 2:6,7). In loving obedience, he chose to fulfill his Father's Will by dying on a cross (Phil 2:8). Because of Jesus' com-plete emptying of himself in love, the Father raised and exalted him! (Phil 2:9). There is a definite build-up in the passage. The climax must be proclaimed clearly and with enthusiasm: Let "every tongue proclaim to the glory of God the Father: JESUS CHRIST IS LORD!" (Phil 2:11).

The gospel is Mark's account of the Passion of our Lord: "It was thus that he humbled himself, obediently accepting even death, death on a cross!" (Phil 2:8)

In the readings, we announce to our brothers and sisters that Jesus is God's Servant, our risen Lord. The Jesus we proclaim is present among us. Our worship today can be the expression of our growing faith awareness of Jesus, as we proclaim "to the glory of God the Father: JESUS CHRIST IS LORD!" (Phil 2:11)

HOLY THURSDAY

Ex 12:1–8, 11–14
1 Cor 11:23–26
Jn 13:1–15

The liturgies of Holy Thursday, Good Friday, and Easter are our three most important celebrations. Our eternal salvation depends on our willingness to accept the events of these three days. Each time we celebrate the Eucharist, we recall and accept Jesus' dying and rising. At the first Eucharist, Jesus looked forward to these two events. In each Eucharist, our Lord, who died and is now risen, is actively present among us and leads us in our celebration.

We come together this evening for a solemn celebration: on the night when our Lord was betrayed, he celebrated the first Eucharist with his close friends and shared his priesthood with them. Today's liturgy recalls how Jesus washed their feet to show that their Christian ministry, in whatever form it takes, must always be an expression of loving service: "What I just did was to give you an example: as I have done, so you must do" (Jn 13:15).

The first reading describes the ritual for the Jewish passover meal. The meal is a memorial feast, recalling the night the angel of destruction "passed over" the houses of the Jews, as they prepared to escape from Egypt. Whenever Jews celebrate the passover meal, they experience a renewed awareness that they belong to God's chosen people. Jesus and his disciples were in the upper room to share this traditional meal. It was on this occasion that Jesus chose to celebrate the Eucharist, the passover meal of the new covenant.

The opening verse of tonight's gospel reading indicates Jesus' attitude at the Last Supper: "Before the feast of Passover, Jesus realized that the hour had come for him to pass from this world to the Father. He had loved his own in this world, and he would show his love for them to the end" (Jn 13:1). Jesus set no limits on his love. He wanted us, his followers, to be God's new people, distinguished by our efforts to serve each other and by our willingness to accept loving service from each other. At the Last Supper, Jesus gave himself completely to his friends: "This is my body, which is for you . . . this cup is the new covenant in my blood" (1 Cor 11:24,25).

This evening, Jesus is among us at our Eucharistic meal. Through the celebrant (concelebrants), he once again takes bread and the cup in his hands, prays the Eucharistic prayer of praise, and shares his sacred meal with us. The words, "This is my body. . . . This is my blood," are a magnificent proclamation. Jesus announces through the priest his victory over Satan, the victory of life over death, the victory of love over sin, the refusal to love. Tonight as we eat our sacred meal, we proclaim the Lord's death, which was his complete giving of himself to the Father and to us (1 Cor 11:26).

GOOD FRIDAY

Is 52:13–53:12
Heb 4:14–16; 5:7–9
Jn 18:1–19, 42

Today's liturgy is perhaps best described as a restrained celebration. As we prayerfully consider our Lord's death and its meaning for us, there is no room for morbid grief. In fact, there are even moments in the Good Friday Service when our joy and gratitude cannot be held back and must be expressed. Without our Lord's death on Good Friday, there would be no joy and hope on Easter

Sunday. Mass is not celebrated today. The Liturgy of the Word begins our worship by inviting us to be responsive to the proclamation of the Good News of salvation in Jesus Christ.

The reading from Isaiah describes the afflictions of the Suffering Servant. Through pain and suffering, the Servant redeems us: "He was pierced for our offenses, crushed for our sins; upon him was the chastisement that makes us whole, by his stripes we were healed" (Is 52:5). "Through his suffering, my servant shall justify many. . . . And he shall take away the sins of many, and win pardon for their offenses" (Is 53:11,12).

When we consider Jesus dying on the cross, in all his anguish and pain, we should not lose sight of what motivated him to undergo such an ordeal. It was love for his Father and for us. In his life, and particularly in his dying, Jesus our Brother experienced our human situation to its fullest: "We do not have a high priest who is unable to sympathize with our weakness, but one who was tempted in every way we are, but never sinned. . . . Son though he was, he learned obedience from what he suffered" (Heb 4:15, 5:8). In his suffering and death, Jesus is both the priest (the one who offers the sacrifice) and the sacrifice. A sacrifice is a gift given to God. Jesus, our high priest, empties himself totally in love to God.

The Passion of John gives an account of the hurried events leading up to our Lord's execution. Jesus' suffering and death are of limitless value because of the love he expressed. As he said his final words, "It is finished" (Jn 19:30), he uttered his full "yes" to God and to us. Through Jesus' death, in his total "yes" which continues in the risen Jesus, we are healed and are reconciled to our Father.

Today we can ask God for the special grace to become more deeply aware of how completely Jesus loves us. Such an awareness can lead us to respond more generously to Jesus who is our hope, "the source of eternal salvation for all who obey him" (Heb 5:9).

**EASTER
VIGIL**

The Easter Vigil is our most important liturgical service in the entire year. Tonight we celebrate the Resurrection of Jesus and the risen life which Jesus shares with us in baptism. We are not just celebrating an event in the past. Our risen Lord is present among us as we celebrate the sacred liturgy.

The seven Old Testament readings and the two readings from the New Testament are carefully selected for proclamation during the Easter Vigil. Each reading helps us gain deeper insight into the mystery of the risen Lord, who fills us with new life in baptism.

Reading I: The long narrative from Genesis proclaims our belief in God who created everything in the world. When the Father raised Jesus from the dead, God's new creation began. In baptism, we are reborn and become new creatures, alive in Jesus.

Reading II: Abraham's willingness to sacrifice his son, Isaac, is an Old Testament foreshadowing of a far greater sacrifice. God our Father has sent his Son, Jesus, who gave himself in the most perfect sacrifice of love.

Reading III: Through God's intervention, the Israelites pass from slavery into new life as God's chosen people. Jesus' Exodus is his passage through death to risen life in full union with his Father. In baptism, our own Exodus, we pass from sin to newness of life in our risen Lord.

Reading IV: To show the intensity of God's love affair with the Israelites, the Old Testament often used the symbolism of the deepest human relationship: the love between husband and wife. In Isaiah, the husband (God) generously continues to love his unfaithful wife (Israel). Like the Israelites, we do not deserve to be loved by God. And yet God loves us intensely as he invites us to be his sons and daughters, baptized in Jesus.

Reading V: God invites the Israelites to come to him to be fulfilled. The risen Jesus, our source of Living Water, invites us to renew the commitment which we made in baptism to place our confidence in him: "Come to me, all you who are weary and find life burdensome, and I will refresh you" (Mt 11:28).

Reading VI: God gave commandments to the Israelites so that, in obeying the commandments, the Israelites would respond in love to God and each other. Our Lord gave us a new commandment: "Love one another as I have loved you." (*See* Jn 13:34.) As we attempt to love each other in this way, the risen Jesus is actually loving other people through us.

Reading VII: Through Ezechiel, God promises to send the Spirit: "I will give you a new heart and place a new spirit within you" (Ez 36:26). In baptism, we receive the Holy Spirit from our risen Lord. The Spirit refashions our hearts and recreates us as the new people of God: "You shall be my people, and I will be your God" (Ez 36:28).

Reading VIII: In baptism, we die with Jesus and rise with him (Rom 6:4). Our dying is a rejection of our old sinful ways. Our rising is our rebirth in the risen Lord. We need not wait until "the last day" to share risen life with Jesus. Right here and now, we are alive with risen life flowing from our Savior!

Reading IX: We waste our time searching for our Lord in an empty tomb. He is risen and lives among us! We are a community, worshipping our Father with Jesus in our midst! Alleluia!

EASTER SEASON

EASTER SUNDAY

*Optional readings:**
Acts 10:34, 37–43
Col 3:1–4, or *1 Cor 5:6–8*
Jn 20:1–9, or *Mt 28:1–10,*
or *Lk 24:13–35*

On Easter Sunday and throughout the Easter Season, we are challenged to deepen our faith in our risen Lord: Do we really believe, with heart and soul, that Jesus has been raised from the dead?

Our first proclamation is a sermon delivered by Peter. It should be proclaimed in that manner. Every sermon is meant to be an exhortation to belief, especially Acts 10, in which Peter urges his listeners to believe in the risen Jesus. Peter speaks "of the way God anointed him (Jesus) with the Holy Spirit and power" (Acts 10:38). The Father's anointing of Jesus as the Messiah was briefly manifested in the Baptism of Jesus: "Suddenly the sky opened and he saw the Spirit of God descend like a dove and hover over him. With that, a voice from the heavens said, 'This is my beloved Son. My favor rests on him'" (Mt 3:16,17). The Father's anointing of Jesus, the Messiah, reaches its climax in the Resurrection. In raising Jesus, the Father fills him with power and the Holy Spirit. (*See* Rom 1:1–3.) Peter states to his listeners that he himself is one of the witnesses who believe in the risen Lord. He is among the "witnesses as had been chosen beforehand by God—by us who ate and drank with him after he rose from the dead" (Acts 10:41).

For the second reading, we have the option to read one of two brief selections from Paul's letters. Col 3:1–4 reminds us of the 8th reading in the Easter Vigil (Rom 6:3–11). We who have been baptized have died with Christ. Our life, though hidden, is truly risen life in Jesus. The second optional reading, 1 Cor 5:6–8, describes how our risen Lord is gradually transforming us from within.

Because of optional readings, it would be helpful for the reader to check in advance which second reading has been selected for the Mass. The remarks in this commentary pertain to Jn 20:1–9 as the third reading.

This transformation occurs especially as we celebrate the Eucharist, Jesus' Passover meal, which he asked us to repeat with our minds and hearts focused on him: "Do this as a remembrance of me" (Lk 22:19).

In Jn 20:1–9, we are told that the "other" disciple (probably John) ran to the tomb with Peter. The "other" disciple "saw and believed" (Jn 20:8). He believed that Jesus who had died on the cross was now raised from the dead. (*See* Acts 10:40.)

Peter and the other early witnesses of the risen Jesus "ate and drank with him after he rose from the dead" (Acts 10:41). We too should approach the Eucharist, our meal with the Lord, willing to have Jesus transform us into true witnesses of his Resurrection.

SECOND SUNDAY OF EASTER

Acts 4:32–35
1 Jn 5:1–6
Jn 20:19–31

Throughout the Easter Season, the selected Scripture readings help us to grow in our awareness that our risen Savior continues to be present and active among us. Our belief in the risen Jesus makes us a unique community. We come together for today's Eucharist to proclaim the hopeful Easter message and to express our willingness to live on peaceful terms with God and with each other.

The early Christians believed that Jesus was still with them. One of the ways in which they expressed this belief was by being responsive to each other's needs. Our first reading describes the closeness experienced by these early Christians: "The community of believers were of one heart and one mind" (Acts 4:32).

In today's second reading, John tells us that we who believe in the risen Jesus are God's children, "begotten by God" (1 Jn 5:1). John indicates that there is but one unmistakable sign that all of us are united in our Father's family—our keeping of God's commandments, especially the loving concern that we show toward our brothers and sisters in need (1 Jn 5:3, 4:20,21).

The opening verse of today's gospel (Jn 20:19) describes the fear and anxiety in Jesus' disciples. They are upset because they feel completely lost without Jesus. But our Lord comforts them by assuring them that he is still with them. Jesus then breathes on them and gives them his Spirit, his precious gift of peace: "Peace be with you!" (Jn 20:19, 21) Jesus challenges his followers to reach out to each other with forgiveness in their hearts. In this way, our Lord's disciples would become his authentic community of believers, at peace with God and with each other.

The risen Jesus whom we proclaim is in our midst as we celebrate the Eucharist today. He sends his Spirit into our hearts so that we too can reach out to one another with kindness and forgiveness. In our Eucharistic prayer, we recommit ourselves to be peacemakers, our Lord's "community of believers . . . of one heart and one mind" (Acts 4:32).

THIRD SUNDAY OF EASTER

Acts 3:13–15, 17–19
1 Jn 2:1–5
Lk 24:35–48

Each and every Sunday, our risen Lord speaks through us as we proclaim the Scripture readings. Today Jesus extends a personal invitation to each of us to open our hearts to the mystery of his dying and rising. He reminds us that he suffered and died in accordance with God's plan: "Everything written about me in the law of Moses and the prophets and psalms had to be fulfilled" (Lk 24:44).

The first reading is part of Peter's sermon to the Jews on Pentecost Sunday. Peter urges his listeners to make the decision to accept Jesus, God's full offer of salvation. God's total love for us, manifested in Jesus' dying and rising, deserves our undivided attention and response:

"Reform your lives! Turn to God, that your sins may be wiped away!" (Acts 3:19)

While dying on the cross, Jesus gave himself in a most complete and generous act of love. In this total giving of self, Jesus became, in person, our perfect sacrifice, entirely pleasing to his Father. Jesus died once and for all (Heb 10:10). But at this very moment, the risen Jesus continues to express his full gift of self to his Father: "We have, in the presence of the Father, Jesus Christ, an intercessor" (1 Jn 2:1). In his very being, Jesus continues to be "an offering for our sins" (1 Jn 2:2). Our Lord helps us to overcome sin in our lives by giving us the strength to love each other as he has loved us (1 Jn 2:10,11).

In the gospel reading we are told that the followers of Jesus did not know how to react to Jesus' death and burial. They were filled with "panic and fright" (Lk 24:37). When Jesus reveals himself to them as risen Lord, they are reassured. They feel "sheer joy and wonder" (Lk 24:41) in their hearts as Jesus explains the Scriptures to them: "He opened their minds to the understanding of the Scriptures . . . that the Messiah must suffer and rise from the dead on the third day" (Lk 24:45,46; Acts 3:18).

Now it is our turn to witness our faith in Jesus whom we proclaim in the readings. He is present among us and enlightens us in "the understanding of the Scriptures" (Lk 24:45). The first followers of Jesus came to know him "in the breaking of bread" (Lk 24:35). We gather today with the sincere hope that in our experience of the Eucharist we too may recognize Jesus present and acting among us.

FOURTH SUNDAY OF EASTER

Acts 4:8–12
1 Jn 3:1,2
Jn 10:11–18

Our prayerful reflection on today's readings can lead us to a deeper understanding of how our risen Saviour is active among us in our Eucharistic celebration. As we proclaim the Scriptures, Jesus sends his Spirit into our hearts to make us aware that we are God's sons and daughters (1 Jn 3:1; *Also see* Rom 8:14–16 *and* Gal 4:6,7). This is the way in which the Spirit of Jesus prepares us for our Eucharistic prayer. With a renewed sense of gratitude, we thank our heavenly Father for his unlimited generosity toward us.

In the first reading, Peter stands before the religious leaders of the Jews to answer their questions about the cure of a crippled man (*See* Acts 3:1–10). Peter shows no fear as he begins his explanation. "Filled with the Holy Spirit" (Acts 4:8), he acknowledges that our risen Lord had acted through him to cure the man. Peter refuses to seek his own glory. He gives Jesus full credit for the cure: "In the power of that name (through Jesus' power) this man stands before you perfectly sound" (Acts 4:10).

Just as only Jesus can perform such a miraculous cure, our eternal salvation is possible only in Jesus "whom you crucified and whom God raised from the dead" (Acts 4:10). We are saved because Jesus died and was raised from the dead by his Father. In baptism, we are united to Jesus in his dying and rising. We died to sin and became alive to God (Rom 6:3,4). Right here and now, we are alive in God's Spirit: "The Spirit of him who raised Jesus from the dead dwells in you" (Rom 8:11). Our salvation has already begun: "We are God's children now" (1 Jn 3:2).

The Holy Spirit lives within us and enlightens us. He helps us to know Jesus more intimately: "I know my sheep and my sheep know me" (Jn 10:14). Getting to know the Lord Jesus means that we come to a deeper appreciation of what it means to be saved by him. Our salvation is entirely a gift: "While we were still sinners, Christ died for us" (Rom 5:8) ; "He first loved us" (1 Jn 4:19).

Today we express our absolute need to be saved by Jesus, "who laid down his life for us" (*See* Jn 10:11). Moved by the Holy Spirit, we give thanks to our Father for the amazing generosity which he has shown us in Jesus: "See what love the Father has bestowed on us in letting us be called children of God! Yet that is what we are" (1 Jn 3:1,2).

FIFTH SUNDAY OF EASTER

Acts 9:26–31
1 Jn 3:18–24
Jn 15:1–8

Many of us have yet to share the exciting experience of worshipping with people who readily show their enthusiasm about coming together to celebrate the Eucharist. And so we decide to conceal our own enthusiasm and settle for quiet and private worship in a crowd of strangers. Perhaps we do not understand that Jesus' command to love also pertains to the manner in which we celebrate the Eucharist: "This is how all will know you for my disciples: your love for one another" (Jn 13:35). The community experience of people being united to each other in him was Jesus' concern as he prayed with his friends at the first Eucharist: "I am the vine, you are the branches" (Jn 15:5).

In today's readings, we proclaim the New Testament challenge to us that we must live and worship together in a genuine Christian community. The first reading describes how the early Christians reacted to Paul's conversion to Jesus. At first they refused to believe that Paul who had been so zealous in persecuting Christians could undergo such a radical change. Then the Spirit removed suspicion from their hearts. "The brothers" (Acts 9:30) warmly accepted Paul in their community. "The church was at peace . . . and enjoyed the increase consolation of the Holy Spirit" (Acts 9:31).

As we grow in our awareness that the risen Jesus lives among us and that we are united in his Spirit, we will sense a greater urgency to reach out to the people who worship around us. We please our heavenly Father when we strive to be aware of each other as we pray the Eucharist: "My Father has been glorified in your bearing much fruit and becoming my disciples" (Jn 15:8). "His commandment is this: we are to believe in the name of his Son, Jesus Christ, and are to love one another as he commanded us" (1 Jn 3:23).

We share a unique experience with each and every person at Mass today. We are all loved by our Father who calls us together to celebrate the Eucharist as his very own people. We express our response to our loving Father both in our love for him and in our love for each other. In today's readings, our Father tells us that he wants us to express our unity as his people: "Little children, let us love one another in deed and truth and not merely talk about it. This is our way of knowing we are committed to the truth and are at peace before him" (1 Jn 3:18,19).

We can honestly say that through our own efforts we have not become much of a community "in deed and truth" (1 Jn 3:18). But "God is greater than our hearts" (1 Jn 3:20). Our risen Lord is present among us and invites us in the gospel to be daring in our prayers (Jn 15:7). Realizing our own shortcomings, we boldly ask our risen Brother to send his Spirit upon us. The Spirit urges us to express more openly and more enthusiastically the love that we have toward each other. In the Spirit of Jesus, we can be transformed into God's worshipping people, brothers and sisters who yearn to live together and pray together in the Lord Jesus.

SIXTH SUNDAY
OF EASTER

Acts 10:25,26, 34,35, 44–48
1 Jn 4:7–10
Jn 15:9–17

During the Easter Season, we celebrate the Resurrection of Jesus. For us, the Resurrection is more than just an event in past history. As believers in the risen Lord, we acknowledge that he is with us each time we come together for the Eucharist.

As risen Lord, Jesus is filled with the Holy Spirit. It is the Spirit who unites Jesus with his Father in their perfect love relationship. At each Eucharistic celebration, Jesus sends this same Spirit of love into our hearts: "As the Father has loved me, so I have loved you" (Jn 15:9). The Spirit of Jesus moves us to love each other with greater generosity. This is the theme of today's Liturgy of the Word: The Spirit of Jesus helps us to love each other as Jesus loved us (1 Jn 4:7; Jn 15:12).

The first reading for last Sunday, the Fifth Sunday of Easter, described how the Holy Spirit moved the early Christians to accept Paul as one of their own. Today's first reading tells us how the Spirit also indicated to the early Christians that they should readily accept non-Jews as fellow believers in Jesus. God, who loves all people, Jews and Gentiles alike, disposes Cornelius and his family to receive the Good News of salvation in Jesus (Acts 10: 1–8). In order to erase all doubt about God's intention to extend the gift of salvation to all people, our risen Lord sends the Holy Spirit upon the new converts: "The circumsized believers . . . were surprised that the gift of the Holy Spirit should be poured out on the Gentiles also" (Acts 10:45). The Jewish Christians then put aside their ethnic resentments and welcomed Cornelius and his household into God's family.

An important indication that we are truly open to the Good News of Jesus is that we place no restrictions on our efforts to love others as Jesus has loved us (Jn 15:12, 17; 1 Jn 4:7). In all our successes and failures to love, we can be inspired by the way God, who is love (1 Jn 4:8), has revealed himself to us: "He sent his only Son to the world that we might have life through him" (1 Jn 4:9). "There is no greater love than this: to lay down one's life for one's friends" (Jn 15:13). When we find it extremely difficult to love others, it is time to remind ourselves that we have never deserved to be loved by God (1 Jn 4:10; Rom 5:8). Yet, despite our unworthiness, Jesus calls us his "friends" (Jn 15:14). Our Lord does not expect us in turn to be restrictive in our love: "Let us love one another because love is of God" (1 Jn 4:7).

As we celebrate today's Eucharist, Jesus sends the Spirit of love into our hearts to break down the "convenient" limits we have set on our love. Do we allow the Holy Spirit to take us by surprise as he did the first Christians? (Acts 10:45) Led by the Spirit in our efforts to become genuine lovers, we proclaim this message to each other: "God shows no partiality" (Acts 10:34).

ASCENSION THURSDAY

Acts 1:1–11
Eph 1:17–23
Mk 16:15–20

Today, as we celebrate Jesus' Ascension into heaven, we consider another aspect of the Easter mystery: Jesus, who died, has been raised to new life by his Father. The glorified Jesus now lives the life of his Father, at the Father's side, "in heaven."

In the second reading, we read Paul's prayerful greeting to the Christians at Ephesus: "May the God of our Lord Jesus Christ, the Father of Glory, . . . enlighten your innermost vision that you may know the great hope to which he has called you" (Eph 1:17, 18). We have good reason to be hopeful because Jesus, our brother, has shown us the way to the Father. "We have such a high priest, who has taken his seat at the right hand of the throne of Majesty in heaven" (Heb 8:1). Jesus' priestly function, his intercession for us, continues in our risen Lord: "Therefore he is always able to save those who approach God through him, since he forever lives to make intercession for them" (Heb 7:25).

In Acts 1:8, Jesus gives his farewell message to his followers: "You are to be my witnesses." We are witnesses of the risen Jesus when our lives proclaim "Alleluia!" to the people around us. We are a believing people who rejoice because Jesus is alive and is still in our midst. Jesus challenges us to believe in his continuing, active presence among us. He acts through us to bring new members into the Church through baptism: "Go into the whole world and proclaim the good news to all creation" (Mk 16:15). That is how we can witness our faith in Jesus who is alive with life from his Father (Jesus is "in heaven.") and, at the same time, is here with us.

It is particularly when we celebrate our meal in commemoration of Jesus' Easter mystery that we should be aware that Jesus is still with us. "So let us confidently approach the throne of grace to receive mercy and favor and to find help in time of need" (Heb 4:16). We can rely on Jesus to be with us. He is our brother, at his Father's side, always interceding for us (Heb 7:25).

SEVENTH SUNDAY OF EASTER

Acts 1:15–17, 20–26
1 Jn 4:11–16
Jn 17:11–19

In our celebration of Ascension Thursday, we renewed our confidence in Jesus our Brother, who "forever lives to make intercession" for us before his Father (Heb 7:25). As he prays before the Father, Jesus continues his presence among us in a mysterious way—"in the Spirit." The risen Jesus first sent his Spirit upon the Church on Pentecost Sunday. In today's Eucharist, we prepare for next Sunday's feast of Pentecost by recognizing our need for the Spirit, who deepens and enriches our faith experience of Jesus.

In our first reading, Peter leads the early Christians as they select Matthias to replace the apostle Judas. Peter describes the important role of an apostle in the community of believers: to be "witness with us to his resurrection" (Acts 1:22). After Matthias becomes an apostle, the stage is set for the Holy Spirit to descend upon the followers of Jesus. On Pentecost, Peter and Matthias and the other ten apostles would openly proclaim the Easter message: "They began to . . . make bold proclamations as the Spirit prompted them" (Acts 2:4).

When Jesus first celebrated the Eucharist with his friends on Holy Thursday evening, he prayed: "O Father most holy, protect them . . . that they may be one, even as we are one" (Jn 17:11). We come together today to celebrate and to express our unity as believers in Jesus. We need each other's support in our efforts to stake our lives on Jesus, our Savior. In our Eucharistic prayer, we seek to deepen our community faith experience of our risen Lord.

On that same Holy Thursday evening, Jesus promised to send us the Spirit to enlighten us: "The Paraclete [Helper] . . . will instruct you in everything" (Jn 14:26). "The Spirit of truth . . . will bear witness on my behalf" (Jn 15:26). The Holy Spirit helps us to see and accept Jesus as our Savior: "We have seen for ourselves . . . that the Father has sent the Son as savior of the world. . . . We have come to know and to believe in the love God has for us" (1 Jn 4:14, 16).

Our risen Lord, filled with the Holy Spirit, is active among us today. If we allow the Spirit to live and move in us, our faith experience of Jesus will be deepened. We approach today's Eucharist by asking Jesus to send his Spirit into our hearts, so that we may be truly his people, "consecrated in truth" (Jn 17:19).

PENTECOST
SUNDAY

Acts 2:1–11
1 Cor 12:3–7, 12,13
Jn 20:19–23

Today's feast, Pentecost, is the great celebration of the birth of the Church. The first Pentecost found the followers of Jesus huddled together, paralyzed with fear. Suddenly they were changed: "All were filled with the Holy Spirit. They began to express themselves in foreign tongues and make bold proclamations as the Spirit prompted them" (Acts 2:4).

We believe that our Savior died and was raised by the Father. Now Jesus is the Messiah, filled with the Spirit. Today we proclaim that the risen Lord continues to send his Spirit upon his Church. The sending of the Holy Spirit by the risen Lord is an important aspect of the Easter mystery.

Like Jesus and the Father, the Holy Spirit is a person veiled in mystery. The Spirit draws the Father and Son together in the beautiful love relationship so often described by Jesus, especially in the gospel of John. When we receive the Holy Spirit, we become brothers and sisters of Jesus. And it is in the same Spirit that we are united to each other as a community of lovers.

The Spirit is active in our lives in many ways. In Paul's letter to the Christians at Corinth, he states that we believe in our risen Lord because the Holy Spirit has been given to us: "No one can say: 'Jesus is Lord,' except in the Holy Spirit" (1 Cor 12:3). Our unity comes from the Spirit: "It is in one Spirit that all of us, whether Jew or Greek, slave or free, were baptized into one body" (1 Cor 12:13). Love is the common language of the Spirit among us (Acts 2:6–11).

In the gospel, the glorified Jesus breathes on his disciples and says: "Peace be with you. . . . Receive the Holy Spirit. If you forgive men's sins, they are forgiven them. . ." (Jn 20:21, 22, 23). Forgiving sins is the work of the Spirit because when our sins are forgiven, we are reconciled to God and to each other in the Church.

Jesus is with us today to lead us in our joyous celebration. The Eucharist is how we express our praise to
the Father for sending the Spirit upon us and for all the
marvelous deeds he has accomplished for us through his
Son (Acts 2:11). Because the spirit is alive in us, we can
approach our Father. Spirited in Jesus, we are able to cry
out, "Abba! Father!" (Gal 4:6).

SUNDAYS IN ORDINARY TIME

1st SUNDAY
IN ORDINARY TIME

See the Feast of the Baptism of the Lord, p. 00

2nd SUNDAY
IN ORDINARY TIME

1 Sm:3:3–10, 19
1 Cor 6:13–15, 17–20
Jn 1:35–42

Before giving our attention to today's three readings, we can briefly consider how readings are selected for the 34 Sundays in Ordinary Time in Cycle "B". Today's second reading is from Paul's first letter to the Corinthians. This particular letter is used in all three Cycles for about six Sundays in Ordinary Time, beginning with the 2nd Sunday. Of the 34 Cycle "B" gospels, 27 are from Mark and seven from John. The Old Testament selection is usually most closely related to the gospel for a given Sunday. But in every Scripture reading, Sunday after Sunday, God speaks to his people as we proclaim the Scriptures.

The theme in today's readings is that as Christians we have a vocation. Our Father personally calls each of us to abandon our sinful ways and to seek life in his Son. Our entire Christian life can be looked upon as our response to this awesome vocation or calling.

In the beginning of Paul's letter to the Corinthians, he reminds these new Christians that they have been "consecrated in Christ Jesus and called to be a holy people" (1 Cor 1:2). Like these early Christians, we can become disheartened by our frequent failures to respond to our vocation. But Paul's words give us encouragement. We will be successful if we are willing to trust in God: "God is faithful, and it was he who called you to fellowship with his Son, Jesus" (1 Cor 1:9).

Our first reading describes God's dramatic call to Samuel. "Samuel answered, 'Speak, Lord, for your servant is listening.' . . . Samuel grew up, and the Lord was with him" (1 Sm 3:9, 19).

In the gospel, Jesus calls his first disciples to take the initial step in their vocation: "Come and see" (Jn 1:39). They follow Jesus and are overjoyed: "We have found the Messiah!" (Jn 1:41)

In the second reading, Paul helps the Corinthians recall that they have been consecrated to Jesus in baptism (1 Cor 6:15). They share the same Spirit of holiness with Jesus (1 Cor 6:17, 19). Therefore, Paul argues, the Corinthians should not slip back into their former practices of lust and immorality (1 Cor 6:16, 18). Like the first Christians at Corinth, we are all called by our Father to accept Jesus. Our calling may not be as dramatic as the calling of Samuel or the calling of Jesus' first disciples. Nevertheless, our Father has called us and continues to call us to deepen our faith in his Son: "Come and see" (Jn 1:39).

Jesus, God's living invitation to us, is present among us at Mass. Our risen Lord comes to invite us to respond to him by discovering how he can fulfill our every need: "What are you looking for?" (Jn 1:38) Jesus challenges us to take all the risks involved in living our faith. He invites us to "let go" of our carefully planned lives and to seek our fulfillment in him: "Come and see" (Jn 1:39).

3rd SUNDAY
IN ORDINARY TIME

Jon 3:1–5, 10
1 Cor 7:29–31
Mk 1:14–20

Repentance, the theme in today's reading, is a definite challenge to us as proclaimers of the Word. For whatever the reasons, in our day and age it seems to be unpopular to stress sin and repentance. Nevertheless, there is nothing theologically outmoded or psychologically harmful in the way that our readings present repentance. Biblically speaking, repentance involves hearing the Good News of God's saving love for us. We manifest our acceptance of the Good News by rejecting sin in our lives and by turning our minds and hearts toward God.

The reading from the prophet Jonah contains a somewhat legendary account of the people of Nineveh being converted to God. Although Jonah's story lacks historical accuracy, we should not miss what the prophet is saying to his Jewish audience. Jonah is, in a subtle manner, making a strong appeal to the religious pride of the Jews: If God were to offer the people of Nineveh the opportunity to repent of their sins, they would readily respond to God. Now if the pagan city of Nineveh would be so willing to turn to God, why shouldn't the Jews, God's chosen people, be ready to do the same? This is Jonah's message to his Jewish listeners.

Mark's gospel gives us a striking summary of our Lord's first sermon: "Jesus appeared . . . proclaiming the good news of God: 'This is the time of fulfillment. The reign of God is at hand! Reform your lives and believe in the good news!'" (Mk 1:15) Whenever Jesus preached, his primary intention was not to give facts and information. First and foremost, Jesus wanted to call attention to himself. Jesus himself is God's Good News. He is personally God's offer of salvation to us. In today's gospel, Jesus is asking his listeners to turn their minds and hearts to him.

In the second reading, Paul is very emphatic about telling the Corinthians and us that we are living in the final phase of history (1 Cor 7:29-31), the time of fulfillment (Mk 1:15). This final era began with the coming of Jesus and climaxes in the events of the Easter mystery: Jesus' dying and rising and his sending of the Holy Spirit into the world. We are now in "the final days." According to the Bible, this last phase of history will draw to a close with the final coming of Jesus, his total victory over sin and death. There will then be the full outpouring of the Spirit of the risen Jesus in the

world. Jesus' Easter mystery will be completely realized
in us, the Church, and in all of creation (Rom 8:19–23).

In today's Liturgy of the Word, we proclaim that God
reveals his full love for us in Jesus. This is certainly good
news for us today, because the risen Jesus, God's Good
News in person, is present among us when we celebrate
the Eucharist. Through our proclamation, our risen Lord
speaks to our brothers and sisters and ourselves. He extends a special invitation to all of us to be converted and
to practice true repentance: To turn our attention toward
him in our midst and to receive him in our hearts: "This
is the time of fulfillment . . . Reform your lives and believe in the Good News!" (Mk 1:15)

4th SUNDAY IN ORDINARY TIME

Dt 18:15–20
1 Cor 7:32–35
Mk 1:21–28

The readings for this Sunday are not easy to understand. Before we consider the overall scriptural theme,
it may be helpful for us to give our immediate attention
to what Paul says in the second reading. Does Paul actually
forbid marriage? He states that he definitely favors the
unmarried state over marriage (1 Cor 7:32–34). In this
passage, however, Paul's main concern is to urge the
Corinthians: "Devote yourselves entirely to the Lord"
(1 Cor 7:35). With the death and Resurrection of Jesus,
history has reached its final phase (Recall last Sunday's
reading from Paul, 1 Cor 7:29–31). Therefore the Christians at Corinth ought to reject once and for all their
former pagan lifestyle, which included an excessive pre-
occupation with sensual matters. A reading of the entire
7th Chapter of 1 Corinthians will convince us that Paul
is not forbidding marriage among the Corinthians. Eph
5:21–33, written at a later date, shows Paul's high esteem
for marriage which he describes as the living sign of the
love relationship between Jesus and us, the Church.

Jesus, God's spokesman to us, is clearly a theme in today's readings: "In times past, God spoke in fragmentary and varied way to our fathers through the prophets; in this, the final age, he has spoken to us through his Son" (Heb 1:1, 2). Jesus is with us as we gather as God's people to celebrate the Eucharist. He comes as risen Lord to teach us with God's full authority. Through the readings, Jesus invites us to open our hearts to what he says to us today.

Throughout the Bible, we read about the prophets, people who acted as God's spokesmen. Prophets do not primarily predict the future, although that is often included in their mission. God speaks to his people through the prophets to make the people aware of his continuing presence among them, and to invite the people to respond to his loving initiatives.

Moses holds a privileged place among Old Testament prophets. In fact, all Old Testament teaching was regarded as somehow originating from Moses. In today's first reading, Moses, God's prophet, is speaking to the Israelites. The chosen people were reluctant to accept Moses as a prophet in their midst. But Moses is persistent in describing the role of a prophet among God's people. Moses also foretells the coming of another prophet.

The gospel passage deals with the question of Jesus' teaching authority. The scribes, the learned religious teachers of Jesus' time, all claimed to teach only by the authority which Moses received from God. Jesus intentionally breaks with this tradition. He acts and teaches as a new Moses, whose authority comes directly from God! Mark reports the amazement of the people who observe what Jesus says and does: "What does this mean? A completely new teaching in a spirit of authority!" (Mk 1:27)

Mark 1:23–25 may be puzzling to us. Why does Jesus silence the unclean spirits who correctly identify him as God's Holy One? (Mk 1:24) Jesus surely did not intend to keep people from believing in him. The secrecy of Jesus' identity is a frequent theme in Mark's gospel. Perhaps in a subtle way Mark is leading his readers, the early

Christian communities and ourselves, to a deeper faith awareness of the real identity of Jesus: "I know who you are—the Holy One of God!" (Mk 1:24)

Our risen Lord is with us today. Without Jesus, we would be imprisoned in the darkness of our own thoughts and ideas. But "the real light which gives light to every man" (Jn 1:9) came into our world. Through Jesus, our heavenly Father reveals his full message of love to us. Jesus teaches us whenever we ponder the meaning of the Scriptures, such as we are doing right now. He teaches us as we proclaim God's Word to our brothers and sisters. Jesus also teaches us how to pray by leading us in our Eucharistic prayer to the Father. Today, let us open our ears and our hearts to Jesus, who is God's spokesman in our midst: "We know who you are—God's Holy One!" (See Mk 1:24)

5th SUNDAY IN ORDINARY TIME

Jb 7:1–4, 6,7
1 Cor 9:16–19, 22,23
Mk 1:29–39

In today's Scriptures, we announce a hopeful theme: Jesus comes to us to bring us the Good News of salvation. Jesus, however, does not choose to arrive in pomp and splendor. He is mysteriously among us in an unassuming manner, "as one who serves" (See Lk 22:27 and Jn 13: 13–17). If we accept Jesus in his servant's role, we can be inspired to be more generous in our own efforts to serve our brothers and sisters.

The Old Testament reading strikes a pessimistic chord. Job is in almost complete despair. He is so wrapped up in self-pity that he cannot see beyond himself. His life seems to drag on and on: "Is not man's life on earth a drugery?" (Jb 7:1) Paradoxically, Job cannot find enough time in life for true enjoyment: "My life is like the wind" (Jb 7:7).

The gospel presents a contrasting scene. Mark's narrative is filled with optimism and joy. Jesus shows his eagerness to make a full commitment to serve people: "Proclaim the good news . . . that is what I have come to do" (Mk 1:38). The demons quickly recognize Jesus as the only authentic, lasting hope for all mankind. "But he would not permit the demons to speak because they knew him" (Mk 1:34; see the commentary on last Sunday's gospel concerning Mark's theme of Jesus' concealed identity). In curing the sick and expelling demons, Jesus performs signs which indicate that he is the long-awaited Messiah. Only by accepting Jesus with faith and confidence can we end our human misery and despair.

In the second reading, Paul testifies to God's strong, persuasive call to him to proclaim hope in Jesus. Paul generously follows God's call and preaches the Good News in a genuine spirit of service. Paul is willing to go to any extreme to make God's offer of salvation in Jesus accessible to everyone: "Although I am not bound to anyone, I made myself the slave of all so as to win over as many as possible" (1 Cor 9:19).

As ministers of God's Word, we too are called to serve others, to be "all things to all men" (1 Cor 9:22). By proclaiming the Scriptures each Sunday, it is our privilege to bring the hopefilled message of salvation to our brothers and sisters. If excessive nervousness or shyness is keeping us from being more effective in our proclamation, perhaps we are too wrapped up in ourselves, as Job was. Perhaps we are not concentrating enough on serving others.

God has called us to perform an awesome task: to serve people by announcing that Jesus is among us. With an enthusiasm mellowed by humility, we accept our task: "Preaching the gospel [Good News] is not the subject of a boast!" (1 Cor 9:16) We are servants of God's people. Our lively proclamation of today's readings can strengthen our faith and the faith of the people who hear us, so that together we will be better prepared to encounter our risen Savior. He is here—the Good News of salvation in person!

6th SUNDAY IN ORDINARY TIME

Lv 13:1,2, 44–46
1 Cor 10:31 – 11:1
Mk 1:40–45

In today's readings, God invites us to deepen our belief in his Son. As we gather to celebrate the Eucharist, the risen Jesus is with us. He comes to bring us hope. Without him, we have no solid reason to be hopeful.

The reading from Leviticus gives an important health directive for the Israelites. In this particular passage and throughout the Bible, we see an intense fear of leprosy. This fear is similar to what many of us feel about contracting terminal cancer or some other incurable disease. There was just no hope for the leper in biblical times. Besides trying to cope with his affliction, a leper among the Israelites had to suffer a more severe punishment: Because of possible contagion, he had to "dwell apart, making his abode outside the camp" (Lv 13:46). He was denied all close contact with the people whom God had chosen as his very own.

One such leper is described by Mark in today's gospel. In his past, there was little cause for hope. Now belief in Jesus begins to stir in the leper's heart. He decides to stake his entire future on Jesus: "If you will to do so, you can cure me!" (Mk 1:40) Jesus lovingly cures the man of his terrible affliction. Our Lord then invites him to observe a ritual in order to give "proof" to the scribes (Mk 1:43, 44). (The scribes, the religious "experts" of that time, refused to believe in Jesus.) The cured man starts on his way to carry out what Jesus commanded him to do. Suddenly he can no longer contain the joy which is exploding in his heart: "The man . . . began to proclaim the whole matter freely, making the story public" (Mk 1:45). He enthusiastically gives praise to God. Strangely enough, Jesus then avoids towns for a while in an attempt not to be recognized (Mk 1:45). In a subtle way, Mark is actually inviting us to believe in Jesus, to "recognize" him as our Savior.

The Jesus whom we believe in is not someone who has lived, died and has "disappeared" into heaven. The risen Jesus is with us today. He invites us to join the eager crowd who keeps "coming to him from all sides" (Mark 1:45). We give glory and praise to our Father (1 Cor 10:31) in today's Eucharistic prayer by expressing our belief that his Son, our hope, is truly among us.

7th SUNDAY IN ORDINARY TIME

Is 43:18,19, 21,22, 24,25
2 Cor 1:18–22
Mk 2:1–12

This Sunday and for the next seven Sundays, the second reading is selected from Paul's second letter to the christian community at Corinth.

Today's three readings closely complement each other to give us the theme for our Mass: In sending Jesus to us, God our Father clearly expresses his full and lasting commitment of love toward us. Our Father invites us to relate to him as his loving sons and daughters. At the end of our Eucharistic prayer, we enthusiastically respond: "Yes! Amen!" (2 Cor 1:20) With our "Great Amen" in today's Mass, we recommit ourselves to our covenant relationship with our Father.

In the reading from Isaiah, God speaks through the prophet and announces that he (God) is ready and willing to renew the Sinai covenant, his love relationship with Israel. The relationship has fallen apart because of Israel's constant infidelity: "You burdened me with your sins" (Is 43:24). God, who initiated the Sinai covenant in the desert, makes still another attempt to gain his people's response: "Your sins I remember no more" (Is 43:25). God urges the Israelites to be so deeply impressed with his new overture of love that they will earnestly strive to respond to him: "See, I am doing something new!" (Is 43:19) But once again the Israelites refuse to be won over by God's loving advances.

Even though most of the Israelites never responded generously to God, God still continued to express his love toward the Israelites and toward all mankind. Finally in Jesus, God made his most complete overture of love toward us: "Whatever promises God has made have been fulfilled in him" (2 Cor 1:20). In Jesus we discover God's perfect and fullest expression of love toward us. Through his life, death and Resurrection, Jesus gives us the opportunity to be forgiven our sins and to be reconciled with our Father. By sending Jesus, God has spoken his total "Yes" to us (2 Cor 1:19). Our Father will never withdraw this commitment. We can count on God who "keeps his word" (2 Cor 1:18).

The gospel begins with a definite sense of urgency: "Word got around that he (Jesus) was at home. At that they began to gather in great numbers" (Mk 2:1, 2). When Jesus delivers God's message to the people, his listeners react differently. Some open their hearts to Jesus, while others, the scribes, remain skeptical. When the people who accept Jesus see him cure the paralyzed man, they are impressed. They suddenly realize that, through the man who stands before them, they can find forgiveness for their sins and reconciliation with God: "They were awestruck; all gave praise to God, saying, 'we have never seen anything like this!'" (Mk 2:12)

Today our Father reaffirms his total commitment of love toward us by sending the risen Jesus to be with us at Mass. Through Jesus we find forgiveness for our sins and reconciliation with our Father. God does not expect us to be sluggish or neutral about what he does for us today in Jesus. Our Father expects us to be "awestruck" (Mk 2:12) in our Eucharistic prayer and to react like the people in today's gospel: "We have never seen anything like this!" (Mk 2:12) With our hearts filled with love and gratitude, we eagerly respond to our Father through Jesus, with Jesus and in Jesus: "It is through him that we address our Amen to God when we worship together" (2 Cor 2:20).

8th SUNDAY
IN ORDINARY TIME

Hos 2:16,17, 21,22
2, Cor 3:1–6
Mk 2:18–22

Today's Scripture readings give us a theme which is similar to the theme we celebrated on the 7th Sunday in Ordinary Time. Once again we prayerfully turn our attention to our covenant with God, our love relationship with the Father of Jesus.

In our Old Testament reading, God speaks to his people in the tender words of the prophet Hosea. Like a husband who yearns to awaken love in his unresponsive wife, God invites the Israelites back "into the desert" (Hos 2:16). The people listening to Hosea are definitely reminded of the Exodus experience of their forefathers. God, however, does not want his people merely to reminisce and become nostalgic about "the good old days." Right here and now, through Hosea, God is inviting the Israelites to respond to his loving advances and to renew the Sinai covenant, the "marriage" between God and his chosen people (*See* Hos, Chapters 1 and 2).

In the gospel, the pharisees and the followers of John the Baptist openly object to the joyful manner in which Jesus attracts his disciples and conducts his ministry: "Why are you and your followers always acting like you are at a party?" (*See* Mk 2:18.) Jesus' reply is simple: "This is the wedding feast!" (*See* Mk 2:19.) Jesus is God's greatest gift to his people. In Jesus, the God of Sinai makes his final and most complete overture of love toward Israel, his spouse.

Through Jesus, God invites us to become more intimate with him. This is the new covenant relationship which God had promised through the prophet Ezechiel: "I will give you a new heart and place a new spirit within you, taking from your bodies your stony hearts. . . . I will put my spirit within you. . . . you shall be my people, and I will be your God" (Ez 36:26, 27, 28).

In today's second reading, Paul compares the Corin-

thian Christians to a loveletter which he has written in
the Spirit of Jesus: "Clearly you are a letter of Christ . . .
written . . . by the Spirit of the living God" (2 Cor 3:3).
Like the Corinthians, we relate to God as our Father,
because the Spirit of the risen Jesus lives within us. Paul
recognizes that he is God's instrument in bringing people
to God through Jesus: "Our sole credit is from God, who
has made us qualified ministers of a new covenant" (2 Cor
3:5, 6).

Today at Mass we celebrate our new covenant relationship with the Father of Jesus. In the three readings,
we proclaim that God's saving love comes to us through
Jesus, who sends his Spirit into our hearts. Like "new
wine" (Mk 2:22), the message of God's love for us is
poured into "new wineskins" (Mk 2:22), our hearts renewed by the Spirit. The risen Jesus is with us today and
sends his Spirit into our hearts. Alive in the Spirit of
Jesus, we respond to our Father in the Eucharistic prayer.
Spirited in Jesus, we cry out: "Abba! Father!" (Gal 4:6)

9th SUNDAY IN ORDINARY TIME

Dt 5:12–15
2 Cor 4:6–11
Mk 2:23 – 3:6 (Long Form),
or Mk 2:23–28 (Short Form)

Today we proclaim an optimistic theme to our brothers and sisters: In the beginning of time, God said: "Let
light shine out of darkness" (2 Cor 4:6; Gn 1:3). Through
Jesus our Savior, God now offers us hope where hope some-
times does not seem possible. Jesus shows us the way to
cope successfully with the difficulties which we face each
day of our lives.

In our Old Testament reading, Moses instructs the
Israelites to refrain from work on the sabbath: "The
seventh day is the sabbath of the Lord, your God. No
work may be done" (Dt 5:14). Moses carefully reminds
the people that, in obeying this commandment, they are

responding to God in the context of the Sinai covenant: "Remember that you too were once slaves in Egypt, and the Lord, your God, brought you out from there with his strong hand" (Dt 5:15).

The pharisees in today's gospel believe they are correct in judging Jesus and his disciples guilty of violating the Jewish sabbath regulations. But what the enemies of Jesus fail to see is that he acts with God's complete authority and sanction: "The Son of Man [Jesus] is lord even of the sabbath" (Mk 2:28). Jesus voices strong opposition to what had become for many Jews a slavish observance of minute religious regulations. But in no way does Jesus ever ridicule the Sinai covenant. He shows his deepest reverence for the love relationship between his Father and Israel by fulfilling all that was promised through Moses and the prophets. Through Jesus, the Sinai covenant is replaced by our new covenant relationship with God as the Father of Jesus (Heb 8:6; Jn 20:17).

In the time of Jesus, every Jew found the strict observance of all religious laws extremely difficult, if not impossible. Jesus does away with this excessive concern for legalistic conformity. Jesus, however, never claimed to make life easy. Like us, he had to face real problems every day of his life: "The pharisees . . . immediately began to plot . . . how they might destroy him" (Mk 3:6).

Jesus did not attempt to escape from the realities of life with all its hardships and struggles. Through his life, death and Resurrection, Jesus succeeded in giving our human experience its deepest meaning. On Good Friday, he faced his own death, the greatest of all human trials. He was arrested, falsely accused and executed. Despite such grossly unfair circumstances, Jesus fully accepted all of what human life entails, including the circumstances of his own death. In Jesus' total "Yes" to his Father, we too can find hope in our lives, even though our problems do not disappear: "We are afflicted . . . but we are not crushed. . . . We are struck down, but never destroyed" (2 Cor 4:8, 9).

Jesus is present among us in our Eucharist today. He

comes as risen Lord, continuing to express his full acceptance of our entire human experience: our delights and
sorrows, our joys and hardships. During our great prayer
of thanksgiving, we join Jesus in saying "Yes" to our
Father in whatever circumstances we find ourselves today.
With no assurance of what tomorrow will bring, with
nothing but trust in our hearts, we accept our Father's
invitation to share mysteriously in the dying and rising of
Jesus: "Continually we carry about in our bodies the
dying of Jesus, so that the life of Jesus may be revealed in
our mortal flesh" (2 Cor 4:11).

10th SUNDAY IN ORDINARY TIME

Gn 3:9–15
2 Cor 4:13 – 5:1
Mk 3:20–35

Because of the disobedience of Adam and Eve, sin is
our inheritance and temptation our constant companion.
Like every member of the human family since Adam and
Eve, we face a daily battle with Satan. Satan is a clever,
deceitful adversary. He employs every possible trick to
fool us. And so it is not surprising that many of our con-
temporaries do not take Satan seriously. Some people claim
that the Devil is not a real personal force in the world.
According to this opinion, Satan is no more than a figurative description of human weakness and failure.

As Christians, we believe that the Devil is real. In
today's readings, we announce this Good News to our
brothers and sisters: Despite Satan's strong influence in
the world, we can find hope in Jesus. With the help of
our Savior, we who are born children of Adam and Eve
can win our lifelong struggle against Satan.

Our Old Testament reading describes some of the con-
sequences of original sin. Satan has clearly won his first
battle with the family of man. But even as darkness and
gloom close in on our first parents, God promises the
dawn of a new day. God promises to send a Savior to

rescue the fallen human race: "He will strike at your
(Satan's) head, while you strike at his heel" (Gn 3:15).
The day would come when Satan would have to wage war
on Eve's offspring, Jesus. Satan would then lose forever
the upperhand which he had gained through the fall of
Adam and Eve.

In today's gospel, some of Jesus' listeners insist that
our Lord is somehow allied with Satan: "He is possessed
by Beelzebul . . . He expels demons with the help of the
prince of demons" (Mk 3:22). Of course, Jesus is irri-
tated and insulted by these remarks. The people who insist on confusing Jesus with Satan are committing blas-
phemy (Mk 3:28–30). They are refusing to accept Jesus
who is in person God's offer of salvation.

In Mk 3:31–35, Jesus is not belittling his mother.
Many early Christian writers used these four verses to
praise Mary as our "New Eve." Graced by God's transforming love, Mary was always obedient to God and completely open to doing his will: "I am the servant of the
Lord. Let it be done to me as you say" (Lk 1:38).

Sin, temptation—and finally death itself come to all
of us through the sin of Adam. Now through Jesus, our
Father offers us the opportunity to live forever: "We believe . . . that he who raised up the Lord Jesus will raise
us up along with Jesus" (2 Cor 4:13, 14). "We have a
dwelling provided for us by God . . . to last forever" (2
Cor 5:1). By dying and rising, Jesus has won for us the
decisive and definitive victory over Satan.

The risen Jesus is with us today in our Eucharistic
celebration. He comes to help us resist Satan who, although defeated, still tries to disrupt our lives. In our
Eucharistic prayer, we recommit ourselves to reject Satan
and to fulfil our Father's will (Mk 3:35). Prayerfully,
we place our trust in what our Father does for us in Jesus:
"We believe . . . that he who raised up the Lord Jesus
will raise us up along with Jesus" (2 Cor 4:13, 14).

11th SUNDAY
IN ORDINARY TIME

Ez 71:22–24
2 Cor 5:6–10
Mk 4:26–34

On the day of our baptism, we made a solemn promise to reject Satan and sin. We committed ourselves to seek a new way of life in the risen Jesus: "You must consider yourselves dead to sin but alive for God in Christ Jesus" (Rom 6:11). Last Sunday, we reflected on the strong influence which the Devil has on our everyday lives. (See the 10th Sunday in Ordinary Time.) The only way that we can overcome Satan is by turning to our Savior. Through Jesus, we can live forever as God's sons and daughters.

God our Father first offered us the amazing gift of lasting life in Jesus when we received baptism. But because many of us were baptized as infants, our parents and God-parents had to express the Christian faith commitment on our behalf. Now as adults, we can no longer depend so totally on the faith of others. To become adult Christians in the fullest sense, we must ratify our baptismal commitment by making our own deliberate decision to accept Jesus as our Savior. In today's Eucharistic celebration, God invites us to renew and re-live our baptismal day.

The theme of today's readings is God's mysterious activity in our lives. In the Bible, God's influence in the world is often referred to as God's Kingdom or Reign. The Kingdom of God has nothing to do with territorial rights. The Bible presents God's Kingdom in an active sense as "God reigning." God's Reign began in our hearts when he touched us with his saving love at our baptism. Our growth in Jesus continues in a gradual, hidden way: "We walk by faith, not by sight" (2 Cor 5:7).

In our first and third readings, Ezechiel and Jesus both use the imagery of growing plants and trees to describe God's mysterious activity in our lives. Speaking through Ezechiel, God promises a new beginning, a rebirth for Israel: "I will . . . tear off a tender shoot, and plant it on a high and lofty mountain. It shall . . . become a majestic cedar" (Ez 17:22, 23, 24). It is not our human prerogative to determine how God must act. Growth in God's Kingdom depends on the power of God, not on our human efforts and insight.

In the gospel, Jesus is speaking to his fellow Jews about God's Reign. As Jesus speaks, a unique moment in Salvation History occurs. Because Jesus is in person God's full offer of salvation to his people, God's Reign reaches its greatest intensity in Jesus. As Jesus speaks to the Jews about God's Reign, he is actually inviting his listeners to accept him as their long-awaited Savior and Messiah. In Jesus, God's Reign reaches its fullest expression.

Today as we gather to celebrate our Eucharist, the risen Jesus, God's Reign in person, is with us. His presence is noticed only by believers. Very inconspicuously, Jesus comes to invite us to deepen our baptismal commitment. We have the opportunity today to make a deliberate decision to belong wholeheartedly to Jesus and to stake our very lives on him. In our Eucharistic prayer, we promise to be faithful to Jesus, to "make it our aim to please him" (2 Cor 5:9). The decision which we express at Mass today affects our eternal destiny: "The lives of all of us are to be revealed before the tribunal of Christ so that each one may receive his recompense" (2 Cor 5:10).

12th SUNDAY IN ORDINARY TIME

Jb 38:1, 8–11
2 Cor 5:14–17
Mk 4:35–41

Our baptismal commitment becomes real only when we are willing to struggle to believe in Jesus in our everyday life situations. Faith is not an easy lifestyle. Like flood waters thundering through a broken dam, trying situations at times get the best of us. Our trust in God

seems to collapse under the strain of our nervous preoc-
cupation with problems. Whenever this happens to us,
we are quick to make excuses: "If I don't worry about my
financial problems, who will?" Or: "What can you expect
when you are forced to deal with 'impossible' people?"
In today's Scripture readings, God invites us to stop making
excuses and to trust in Jesus.

Today's first reading is taken from one of the most
interesting books of the Old Testament. Repeatedly,
Job has had to face severely trying situations. Job's three
friends persist in giving him advice. This merely creates
more worry and confusion in Job. Finally in desperation,
Job sees no other alternative but to demand an explanation from God (*See* Jb, Chapter 31). God gives Job an
unexpected reply: "Where were you when I founded the
earth?" (Jb 48:4) God is in control of everything in the
world, even the mighty forces unleashed by the stormy
sea: "Who shut within doors the sea, when it burst forth
from the womb?" (Jb 38:8) God is not required to answer
to Job or to anyone else. In humble submission, without
the answers he once sought, Job expresses his trust in God:
"I know that you can do all things. . . . I have dealt with
great things that I do not understand" (Jb 42:2, 3).

The gospel describes the complete panic of Jesus' dis-
ciples: "We are going to drown!" (Mk 4:38) Then to
their utter amazement, the disciples see God's power at
work in Jesus. With an effortless gesture and a few words,
Jesus calms the raging sea: "Quiet! Be still!" (Mk 4:39)
Then Jesus turns to his followers and challenges them:
"Why are you so terrified? Why are you lacking in faith?
A great awe overcome them at this" (Mk 4:41).

In the second reading, Paul chides the Christians at
Corinth. Instead of constantly making excuses for not
living out their Christian belief, they should be strongly
motivated by Christ's love for them (2 Cor 5:14). This
love, Paul writes, "impels us who have reached the conviction that. . . . he died . . . so that we might no longer
live for ourselves, but for him. . . . If anyone is [alive]
in Christ, he is a new creation" (2 Cor 5:14, 15, 17). The

old order, filled with worries that control us and consume our time, "has passed away" (2 Cor 5:17).

We are so much like the people in today's readings: Job, the Corinthians and the terror-stricken disciples of Jesus. We too are a people easily disturbed by change. Our faith is weak. We are quick to panic, quick to complain to God when we face adversity and hardship.

Today in our Eucharistic celebration, the risen Jesus comes among us to calm us down, just as he once calmed the sea and his fearful disciples. Jesus comes not to "explain away" our problems. Our Lord merely asks us to trust in him. Filled with awe at the power of Jesus, we support each other as we attempt to discover Jesus in our midst and to accept him as the Lord of our lives: "Who can this be that the wind and the sea obey him?" (Mk 4:41)

13th SUNDAY IN ORDINARY TIME

Wis 1:13–15, 2:23,24
2 Cor 8:7, 9, 13–15
Mk 5:21–43 (Long Form),
or Mk 5:21–24, 35–43 (Short Form)

In today's readings, our Father invites us to deepen our belief in Jesus. Today, as in every Eucharistic celebration, we are faced with a decision: If we choose to be deceived by the false attractions of sin, we will be led to death and eternal failure (*See* Wis 2:24). If, on the other hand, we choose to place our trust in our risen Savior, we will live forever in him.

In our second reading, Paul writes to the Christian community at Corinth and reminds the Corinthians of the beautiful gift which God offers us in Jesus: "For your sake he made himself poor though he was rich, so that you might become rich by his poverty" (2 Cor 8:9). St. Augustine and other writers in the early Church were amazed by this same realization: Jesus became our human brother, so that we might become like him, alive with God's life. At the end of the second reading, Paul asks the Corinthians to demonstrate their appreciation for

God's generosity by sharing whatever wealth they possess (2 Cor 8:13–15).

Decisions play an important part in today's gospel. When Jesus entered Jairus' home to cure his daughter, some people decide to ridicule Jesus (Mk 5:40). In contrast, the gospel relates two inspiring examples of people who make decisions to trust completely in Jesus. The woman whom Jesus cured tells him "the whole truth" (Mk 5:33), the moving story of her total trust in Jesus. Jesus also finds great faith and confidence in the family of Jairus. Our Lord rewards their trust well beyond their expectations: "The girl . . . stood up immediately and began to walk around. At this the family's astonishment knew no bounds" (Mk 5:42).

Our life-giving Savior comes among us in our Eucharistic celebration. In order to receive the richness of risen life from Jesus, we have to admit our utter poverty. All of us, rich and poor, must decide to go empty handed to Jesus in order to receive lasting life from him.

14th SUNDAY IN ORDINARY TIME

Ez 2:2–5
2 Cor 12:7–10
Mk 6:1–6

God our Father speaks to us in a very human way—through the words and actions of other people. At baptism, God called each of us to be his spokesman. In our sincere efforts to respond to this prophetic calling, we become a resounding, joyfilled Alleluia, a living proclamation that the risen Jesus is alive and active in the world today.

This Sunday's readings describe the roles of three prophets among God's people: Ezechiel, Paul and Jesus, who is God's Word in person. Like all prophets, they had to struggle to be faithful in their prophetic mission. Today's scriptural theme, the struggles in the life of a prophet, can be especially inspirational to us who are lectors. Each Sunday, God depends on us to proclaim the Good News of salvation in Jesus. Each Sunday, through our proclamation, our heavenly Father invites his people to respond to his love in the Eucharist, our great prayer of praise and thanksgiving.

In our first reading, God sends Ezechiel to be his prophet among the Israelites. No easy task is in store for Ezechiel: "Hard of face and obstinate of heart are they to whom I am sending you" (Ez 2:4). Through Ezechiel, God intends to invite his people to repent and to be reconciled to him in the Sinai love relationship: "You shall be my people, and I will be your God." (Ez 36:28). God asks Ezechiel to be brave. He is to stand among resentful people and announce God's message to them: "This is the Word of the Lord! Thus says the Lord God!" (Ez 2:4)

In the gospel reading, Jesus, God's Incarnate Word, speaks to the Israelites: "In times past, God spoke in fragmentary and varied ways to our fathers through the prophets; in this, the final age, he has spoken to us through his Son" (Heb 1:1, 2). But even Jesus, God's prophet par excellence, does not receive a welcoming response from many of his listeners: "They found him too much for them" (Mk 6:3). The people are quick to respond to Jesus with prejudiced minds: "Where? . . . What? . . . Why?" (Mk 6:2, 3)

Paul is an important New Testament prophet whom God used to spread the Good News of Jesus to cities throughout the Roman Empire. In today's second reading, Paul humbly confides in the Christians at Corinth. By experiencing his own weakness, Paul now has a new awareness of God's strength: "I willingly boast of my weakness . . . that the power of Christ may rest upon me" (2 Cor 12:9).

We have no reason to assume that our task as lectors should be easy. We have to pray, prepare and practice with diligence in order to proclaim the Good News of salvation in Jesus to our brothers and sisters. Like Paul, we have to admit our weakness so that we will be fit instruments of God's Word: "When I am powerless, it is then that I am strong" (2 Cor 12:10).

The risen Jesus, whom we proclaim, comes among us today to lead us in our Eucharistic prayer. Our task as lectors is prophetic. We are God's spokesmen, preparing our brothers and sisters and ourselves to encounter in faith the risen Jesus in our midst today.

15th SUNDAY IN ORDINARY TIME

Am 7:12–15
Eph 1:3–14 (Long Form),
or Eph 1:3–10 (Short Form)
Mk 6:7–13

Beginning today and for the next five Sundays, the second Scripture reading is taken from Paul's letter to the Christians at Ephesus.

Last Sunday's theme is closely related to today's theme. Last Sunday we considered how God speaks to his people through prophets. The prophets mentioned in today's readings are Amos, Paul, Jesus' Apostles and finally Jesus, in whom God fully expresses his Word in our human situation. All prophets are called to the task of proclaiming the message of God's love for his people. By their persistent, enthusiastic proclamation, prophets invite people to respond to God's love.

In our Old Testament reading, Jeroboam, King of Israel, and the priest Amaziah are threatened by Amos' prophetic words and actions. Amaziah attempts to banish Amos from the temple area. But God's prophet refuses to be intimidated: "I was no prophet . . . The Lord took me from following the flock, and said to me, 'Go, prophesy to my people Israel. Now hear the word of the Lord!' " (Am 7:14, 15, 16)

In the gospel, Jesus commissions "the Twelve" to preach in his name. Through their prophetic words and actions (Mk 6:12, 13), the apostles are to bring people to Jesus by their announcement that God's kingdom has arrived in the person of Jesus. Jesus' advice to his apostles is harsh, but realistic: Since Jesus himself has not been ac-

cepted by all his listeners, it is foolhardy for his apostles to
expect greater success.

As lectors, we do far more than bring people information about God. God speaks to his people through us!
If we are dull in our approach to the Scriptures, we will
discourage people from responding to God. But if we are
deeply impressed by God's message of love and communi-
cate our enthusiasm in our proclamation, then we will
encourage our brothers and sisters to respond to God. In
proclaiming God's Word, we must be as intense as a
husband who, in the intimacy of passionate lovemaking,
moves his wife to a joyfilled response to him. Today we
stand before God's people to proclaim the Good News of
Jesus and to invite the people to make loving responses to
God in the Eucharistic prayer.

Paul's outburst of praise to our heavenly Father (Eph
1:3–14) lends itself well to our enthusiastic proclamation.
Our Father expresses his saving love for us in his Son:
He "predestined us through Christ Jesus to be his adopted
sons . . . that all might praise the glorious favor he has
bestowed on us in his beloved" (Eph 1:5, 6). In this
beautiful prayer of praise, Paul suggests the loving response
which our Father expects us to express in our Eucharistic
prayer.

The risen Jesus, the Father's Beloved, is with us today. As we proclaim the Scriptures, Jesus sends the Holy
Spirit into our hearts. Alive in the Spirit of Jesus, we
pray our Eucharistic prayer with our hearts overflowing
with enthusiasm: "Praised be the God and Father of our
Lord Jesus Christ, who has bestowed on us in Christ every
spiritual blessing in the heavens!" (Eph 1:3)

16th SUNDAY IN ORDINARY TIME

Jer 23:1–6
Eph 2:13–18
Mk 6:30–34

Whenever we Roman Catholics reflect on the shepherd theme in the Bible, we seem to lull ourselves into

a false sense of security. The text which makes us most
comfortable is Jn 10:16: "I have other sheep that do not
belong to this fold. I must lead them, too, and they shall
hear my voice. There shall be one flock then, one shepherd." From this text, we immediately presume that we
comprise Jesus' true fold and we consider all non-Catholics
to be outside "our" fold. Our prayer for non-Catholics
is rather smug: We ask that they will one day see the light,
embrace the Catholic faith and enter into full communion
with Jesus and with us. We are so sure of our position
that we expect Protestants to understand why we are condescending toward them. Our smugness, however, does
little more than give Protestants a solid reason for con-
cluding that Catholics worry first about church member-
ship and only secondarily about humbly accepting Jesus
as our Savior.

Today's Liturgy of the Word shakes us out of our
complacency and challenges our condescending attitude
toward non-Catholics. The theme of the readings is that
Jesus is our Shepherd and our Peacemaker. It is only when
all Christians earnestly seek Jesus as Shepherd and Peacemaker that we can hope to be united to each other and
fully reconciled to our heavenly Father.

In the first reading, God expressed his displeasure
with the leaders of his people: "You have scattered my
sheep. . . . I myself will gather the remnant of my flock
from all the lands" (Jer 23:2, 3). God promises to send
a new King, a descendant of David, to shepherd his people
(Jer 23:5, 6). Jesus is the fulfilment of this promise:
"Jesus saw a vast crowd. He pitied them, for they were
like sheep without a shepherd" (Mk 6:34). Jesus came to
announce "the Good News of Peace" (Eph 2:17) and to
bring reconciliation to people who open their hearts to
his Good News.

In contrasting Jews and Gentiles, Paul considers all
of mankind: Jews as "near by" and Gentiles as "far off"
(Eph 2:13). To find true reconciliation with each other,
all of us must be willing to turn to Jesus: "Through him
we . . . have access in one Spirit to the Father" (Eph 2:18).

At the Last Supper, Jesus told his followers: "No one comes to the Father but through me" (Jn 14:6). Our Father is not being arbitrary or limiting by making Jesus our sole access to himself. Jesus is God's Son, the Father's perfect manifestation of love. The Father gives himself to us completely in Jesus. By dying and rising, Jesus paid the full price of reconciliation. Now as risen Lord, Jesus sends his Spirit into our hearts to lead us all to his Father.

It is not our primary task today to pray for Protestants. Rather we should look first at ourselves and discover the areas in which we are closed to the Spirit of Jesus. If we are honest with ourselves, we will see that we are not yet the people our Father calls us to be. We are still strangers to ourselves, distant from each other and not fully reconciled to our Father. We need the Spirit of Jesus to enjoy lasting peace and reconciliation.

The risen Jesus is with us in today's Eucharistic celebration. He sends the Spirit into our hearts so that we can end our hostility and be reconciled to God: Through Jesus, our Peacemaker, we "have access in one Spirit to the Father" (Eph 2:18).

17th SUNDAY IN ORDINARY TIME

2 Kgs 4:42–44
Eph 4:1–6
Jn 6:1–15

Mark's gospel is generally used on "Cycle B" Sundays. From the 17th Sunday through the 21st Sunday in Ordinary Time, however, our gospel reading will be taken from the 6th Chapter of John.

In 2 Kings, God works through Elisha, who is described as "a man of God" (2 Kgs 1:9). God shows that he cares for his people by miraculously feeding a hundred men with twenty small barley loaves. God invites his people to trust totally in him for their needs: "When they had eaten, there was some left over" (2 Kgs 4:44).

God our Father expresses his greatest love and care

for us through his Son: "Jesus looked up and caught sight of a vast crowd coming toward him" (Jn 6:5). Jesus then feeds five hundred people with five barley loaves and two dried fish. "When they had had enough. . . . they gathered twelve baskets full of pieces left over" (Jn 6:12, 13). Excitement buzzes through the crowd. The people see Jesus as the fulfilment of their hopes and dreams. They hasten to make Jesus their leader, according to their impression of "the prophet who is to come into the world" (Jn 6:14). Jesus hurries away "to the mountain alone" (Jn 6:15) so that the people will not misrepresent his mission. He came to reveal his loving, caring Father to us (Jn 1:18) and to bring us life "in abundance" (Jn 10:10).

In our second reading, Paul urges the Christian community at Ephesus to be faithful to God's calling: "Make every effort to preserve the unity which has the Spirit as its origin and peace as its binding force" (Eph 4:3). Paul then reminds the Ephesians that "There is but one body and one Spirit . . . one hope. . . . one Lord, one faith, one baptism; one God and Father of all" (Eph 4:4, 5, 6).

As we gather for the Eucharist today, our risen Brother is with to us help us celebrate our unity as our Father's people. With one mind and heart, we join together in our Eucharistic prayer of praise. Spirited in Jesus, we express our total confidence in our Father, "who is over all, and works through all, and is in all" (Eph 4:6).

18th SUNDAY IN ORDINARY TIME

Ex 16:2–4, 12–15
Eph 4:17, 20–24
Jn 6:24–35

All of us who have decided to accept Jesus as our Savior face the daily danger of becoming pagans. Each day of our lives, we are tempted to confuse genuine trust in Jesus with the comfort we feel in using a routine religious practice or a regular set of prayers. Without realizing it, we seek ways to dispense ourselves from authentic faith in Jesus. We would like to accept Jesus on our own terms, rather than on God's terms. In today's readings, our Father asks us to end our search for phony faith substitutes and to trust totally in his Son.

In the second reading, Paul writes to the Ephesians and contrasts two lifestyles: pagan and Christian. Pagans act like dandelion fluff being blown about on a windy day. Pagans go through life in an "empty headed" (Eph 4:17), purposeless way that leads to self destruction. By contrast, belief in Jesus means that we enjoy continual growth in him. Paul urges the Ephesians to reject once and for all the pitfalls of paganism: "You must lay aside your former way of life. . . . and put on that new man created in God's image" (Eph 4:22–24).

Today's Old Testament reading finds the Israelites grumbling against Moses and Aaron. The chosen people have forgotten the love which God had shown them in delivering them from Egyptian bondage. They are certain that God has tricked them: "Would that we had died at the Lord's hand in the land of Egypt, as we . . . ate our fill of bread! But you had to lead us into the desert to make the whole community die of famine!" (Ex 16:3) In reply, God reinforces his demand that the Israelites learn to trust in him each day of their lives: "I will now rain down bread from heaven for you. Each day the people are to go out and gather their daily portion" (Ex 16:4).

In the gospel, the crowd who had been miraculously fed by Jesus (Jn 6:1–13) eagerly chases after him. Jesus takes advantage of this unusual situation to invite the Jews to seek another kind of nourishment: belief in him! "You should not be working for perishable food but for food that remains unto life eternal. . . . Have faith in the One whom he [the Father] sent" (Jn 6:27, 29). The Jews insist that they need constant reassurance, a continuing sign like the heavenly-sent manna. Jesus challenges them to stop thinking of bodily nourishment and to risk the leap of faith. His listeners are slow to understand what Jesus means. They ask for a bread which they can eat every day of their lives: "Give us this bread always" (Jn 6:34).

Jesus again invites the crowd to believe in him and be thoroughly satiated: "I myself am the bread of life. No one who comes to me shall ever be hungry, no one who believes in me shall thirst again!" (Jn 6:35)

The same Jesus who invited people to belief in the gospel passage is with us today as we celebrate the Eucharist. The risen Jesus says to each one of us: "No one who comes to me shall ever be hungry, no one who believes in me shall thirst again!" (Jn 6:35) Are we willing to put aside our attempts to find convenient escape hatches and to stake our lives completely on Jesus?

19th SUNDAY IN ORDINARY TIME

1 Kgs 19:4–8
Eph 4:30 – 5:2
Jn 6:41–51

Today we proclaim a message of hope to our brothers and sisters. At times our problems can be so overwhelming that we are tempted to give up. In this Sunday's Scripture readings, our Father invites us to deepen our belief in Jesus and to find new strength in him.

Our first reading describes Elijah in a state of depression. He sees no reason to go in life: "He prayed for death: 'This is enough, O Lord! Take my life'. . . . He lay down and fell asleep" (1 Kgs 19:4, 5). But God does not abandon Elijah and gives the prophet strength which he never expected to receive.

In today's gospel, the Jews are perplexed because Jesus has asked them to place their complete trust in him (See the 18th Sunday in Ordinary Time). They claim to know everything there is to know about Jesus: "Is this not Jesus, the son of Joseph? Do we not know his father and mother? How can he claim to have come down from heaven?" (Jn 6:42) The Jews fail to recognize that Jesus enjoys a unique relationship with God. On the night of the Last Supper, Jesus said: "I did indeed come from the

Father. I came into the world. Now I am leaving the world to go to the Father" (Jn 16:28).

The Jews in today's gospel see Jesus in competition with their God. But Jesus explains over and over again that he is "the One sent by the Father" (Jn 6:29, 38, 39, 44). He is the Son of the God of Sinai. The Father fully supports everything that Jesus says and does. In fact, in a mysterious manner, it is the Father who calls people to Jesus: "No one can come to me unless the Father who sent me draws him. . . . Everyone who has heard the Father and learned from him comes to me" (Jn 6:44, 45).

Jesus is the Father's Beloved, the perfect manifestation of God's love in our world of human experience (Jn 3:16). In sending Jesus, God makes his definitive commitment of love toward us. To reach lasting life with our Father, we must accept the Father's invitation and believe in Jesus: "No one comes to the Father but through me" (Jn 14:6). "He who believes [in Jesus] has eternal life (Jn 6:47). "I myself am the bread of life. . . . If anyone eats this bread he shall live forever" (Jn 6:51). Jesus fully reveals his Father's saving love for us when he died on the Cross: "It is precisely in this that God proves his love for us: that while we were still sinners, Christ died for us" (Rom 5:8). "He gave himself for us as an offering to God" (Eph 5:2). "The bread I will give is my flesh, for the life of the world!" (Jn 6:51).

Our Father sends his Son to us as we celebrate today's Eucharist. The risen Jesus comes among us to continue his perfect act of self-giving which he expressed in his death on the cross (Eph 5:2). But we are not to be passive spectators at Mass today. Our Father draws us and invites us to grow stronger in our faith relationship with Jesus. Responding to our heavenly Father's invitation, we pray the Eucharist in a way that is most pleasing to our Father—through Jesus, with Jesus and in Jesus!

20th SUNDAY
IN ORDINARY TIME

Prv 9:1–6
Eph 5:15–20
Jn 6:51–58

Today, for the fourth consecutive Sunday, the gospel reading is taken from the 6th Chapter of John. On the 17th Sunday in Ordinary Time, our Father invited us to trust in his loving care for us. On the 18th and 19th Sundays, our Father asked us to deepen our faith in his Son. In today's readings, God invites us to believe in Jesus, who makes a total and complete gift of himself to us in our Eucharistic meal.

Because we rarely compare the four gospels, it is probably surprising to realize that John does not follow the lead of the other three evangelists in narrating Jesus' institution of the Eucharistic meal (*See* Mt 26:26–30; Mk 14:22–26; Lk 22:14–20). Even Paul, who was not present at the Last Supper, describes what Jesus did "on the night in which he was betrayed" (*See* 1 Cor 11:23–26). Although John does not narrate Jesus' sacred action at the Last Supper, he presents the Eucharist to us in a different setting. In today's gospel (Jn 6:51–58), Jesus extends an awesome invitation to his first followers and to us. He invites us to the Eucharistic table to eat his flesh and drink his blood.

In Proverbs, two kinds of wisdom are contrasted: God-given wisdom and wisdom obtained by human insight alone. Personified in figurative terms, Divine Wisdom invites the Israelites to be wise in the Lord. Whoever does not seek God's Wisdom is foolish: "Forsake foolishness that you may live; advance in the way of understanding" (Prv 9:6). Wisdom invites us to share a most intimate meal with her: "She has spread her table. . . . 'Come, eat of my food, and drink of the wine I have mixed!' " (Prv 9:2, 5) In order to taste of God's Wisdom, we have to admit that we cannot gain this Wisdom by our own powers of concentration. The reward for our humility is more than we can imagine: We will come to know God in a deeply intimate way.

Jesus, the fulness of God's revelation to us, is God's Wisdom in person! Like Wisdom in the first reading, Jesus beckons the people in the gospel and us: "Come, eat of my food!" With unrestrained generosity, Jesus gives us his own Body and Blood for our meal. In so doing, Jesus gives himself to us completely and invites us to be on very intimate terms with him: "He who feeds on my flesh and drinks my blood has life eternal. . . . Just as the Father who has life sent me and I have life because of the Father, so that man who feeds on me will have life because of me" (Jn 6:54, 57).

Once again at our Mass today, Jesus does what he did in the Cenacle Room. Acting through our celebrant, our risen Lord prays over bread and wine. Through the power of Jesus, bread and wine truly become his Body and Blood. Bread and wine are the sacred signs of Jesus' total self-gift to us: "This is my body . . . given for you! This cup is the new covenant in my blood . . . shed for you!" (Lk 22:19, 20)

How can we even begin to express our gratitude to our Father for inviting us to our Eucharistic meal? At Mass the risen Jesus changes not only bread and wine. He also sends his Spirit to transform our hearts so that we will be able to offer enthusiastic Eucharistic praise to our Father: "Be filled with the Spirit, addressing one another in psalms and hymns and inspired songs. Sing praise to the Lord with all your hearts. Give thanks to God the Father always and for everything in the name of our Lord Jesus Christ" (Eph 5:18–20).

21st SUNDAY IN ORDINARY TIME

Jos 24:1,2, 15–17, 18
Eph 5:21–32
Jn 6:60–69

Today we complete the sequence of the five Sundays having gospel readings taken from John 6. In this Sunday's readings, our Father asks us to be decisive about seeking salvation in Jesus: "Decide today whom you will serve" (Jos 24:15).

Making the important decision to recommit ourselves to Jesus should not be taken lightly. In the first reading, Joshua has succeeded Moses as the leader of the wandering Israelites. Joshua invites the people to make a solemn recommitment of themselves to God in the Sinai love relationship. The Israelites say "yes" to God in their liturgy, but many among the chosen people never lived out this commitment.

In our Eucharistic celebration today, we rededicate ourselves to our life-long task of discovering the risen Jesus in our midst—in the breaking of bread and in the closeness witnessed by married couples in our worshipping community. When we stop to think of it, it is utterly amazing that Jesus wished to be so intimately involved in our lives. In our sharing of our Eucharistic meal, Jesus shares himself totally with us. Jesus also wishes to reveal himself in the love relationship between husband and wife: "A man shall leave his father and mother, and shall cling to his wife, and the two shall be made into one" (Eph 5:31; Gn 2:24). For married couples, clinging to each other is their way to cling to Jesus. Because of the generosity expressed in their marital love, all of us in the larger Eucharistic community can be inspired to recommit ourselves to cling to our Savior.

In our second reading, Paul tells us that a married couple, in manifesting their mutual love, give a living sign of the love relationship between Jesus and us, the Church. This sacramental witness of a married couple becomes real only when both husband and wife make explicit faith decisions. Every act of love is a decision. For a husband to love his wife as Jesus loved the Church (Eph 5:25), he must be convinced of the total outpouring of love expressed by the dying Jesus. It is only when a husband makes such a total commitment to love his wife that she can be expected to decide to respond wholeheartedly to him: "Wives should be submissive to their husbands as if to the Lord" (Eph 5:22). A wife responds to her husband just as we, the people of Jesus, respond to the love which Jesus has expressed for us in his living, dying and rising. There is no genuine expression of marital love unless husband and wife are deeply committed to finding Jesus' saving love in each other. In marriage, two lovers, filled with Jesus' Spirit of love, free each other from the shackles of selfishness and discover the Lord Jesus in their midst, in their relationship. In the love shared between husband and wife, Jesus shares himself with the married couple. Jesus' saving love touches the husband through his wife. Jesus' saving love touches the wife through her husband. The risen Jesus, who creates love in our lives, creates the beautiful sign of a husband and wife in love.

The risen Jesus comes among us today as we celebrate our Eucharist. Jesus invites us to discover him in faith in the intimacy of marital love and in our Eucharistic meal. Responding with the enthusiasm of Simon Peter, we recommit ourselves to finding the Lord Jesus in our midst: "Lord, to whom shall we go? You have the words of eternal life" (Jn 6:68).

22nd SUNDAY IN ORDINARY TIME

Dt 4:1–2, 6–8
Jas 1:17,18, 21,22, 27
Mk 7:1–8, 14,15, 21–23

Today we begin selections from the letter of James as our second reading. Through our proclamation of today's readings, God invites us to open our hearts to his Word, "with its power to save us" (Jas 1:21).

In the Old Testament reading, Moses speaks to the Israelites: "Now, Israel, hear the statutes and decrees which I am teaching you" (Dt 4:1). In the apostle James' letter, he exhorts the early Christians: "Humbly welcome the word that has taken root in you" (Jas 1:21). In the gospel, Jesus "summoned the crowd again and said to them: 'Hear me, all of you, and try to understand. . . .

Let everyone heed what he hears!' " (Mk 7:14, 16)

As we might expect, the Bible tells us a great deal about God's Word. In a striking passage, the prophet Isaiah poetically describes how God speaks to us. God's Word comes forth from God and then returns to God. Isaiah compares God's Word to rain and snow which water the soil to make it productive (Is 55:10). "So shall my word be that goes forth from my mouth; it shall not return void, but shall do my will, achieving the end for which I sent it" (Is 55:11).

To prepare the Israelites for the coming of Jesus, God spoke to them with impressive words and actions. In Deuteronomy, Moses reminds the people of how God had lovingly rescued them from Egyptian slavery and made them his very own people: "What great nation is there that has gods so close to it it as the Lord, our God?" (Dt 4:7) God's loving actions on behalf of his people demanded a response from them. Moses instructs the Israelites to give their response to God in the context of their obedience to the commandments: "Israel, hear the statutes and decrees which I am teaching you to observe" (Dt 4:1).

In Jesus, God makes his most complete gesture of love toward his people. In Jesus' words and works, God speaks his final word to the Israelites. Nevertheless, Jesus finds his listeners responding in a strange manner. Instead of opening their hearts to accept Jesus, "the experts in the law" (Mk 7:1) criticize him. But Jesus continues to try over and over again to get his Father's beloved people to make a loving response: "Hear me . . . and try to understand" (Mk 7:14).

James writes to people who have already accepted the message of salvation in Jesus. But just hearing words is not enough: "Act on this Word. If all you do is listen to it, you are deceiving yourselves" (Jas 1:22). God's Word must reach others through the generous witness of Christians: "Looking after orphans and widows in their distress and keeping oneself unspotted by the world make for pure worship without stain before our God and Father" (Jas 1:27).

God speaks to our brothers and sisters today as we read the Scriptures. In our proclamation, God's message of love in person, the risen Jesus, becomes present among us. Our risen Brother sends his Spirit into our hearts so that we can respond to our Father with enthusiastic praise in our Eucharistic prayer: "So shall my word be that goes forth from my mouth; it shall not return void, but shall do my will, achieving the end for which I sent it" (Is 55:11).

23rd SUNDAY
IN ORDINARY TIME

Is 35:4–7
Jas 2:1–5
Mk 7:31–37

In today's Mass we celebrate a hopeful theme: Jesus comes among us to open our eyes and ears. If we are daring enough to believe in the power of our risen Savior, we will be amazed at the changes which take place in our lives. We will see what we have been previously blind to and we will hear what we have never heard before. "Here is your God. . . . he comes to save you. Then will the eyes of the blind be opened, the ears of the deaf cleared" (Is 35:4, 5).

In the gospel passage, Jesus opens the ears of a deaf man and at the same time frees him of a speech impediment. The crowd becomes wild with enthusiasm: "Their amazement went beyond all bounds: 'He has done everything well! He makes the deaf hear and the mute speak!'" (Mk 7:37)

In the second reading, James tries to show the early Christians the inconsistency of claiming that they believe in the risen Jesus while continuing to judge people by appearance alone. "Have you not . . . discriminated in your hearts? Have you not set yourselves up as judges handing down corrupt decisions?" (James 2:4)

Today we gather with our brothers and sisters to pray the Eucharist. Do we really believe that the risen Jesus is in our midst and lives in each and every person in our

worshipping community? Or do we persist in judging people by our first impression of them? None of us can ever
see beyond appearances without the help of Jesus. Today,
Jesus invites us to turn to him to be cured of our many
"blind spots." Jesus comes to cure any of us who are
humble enough to ask to be cured. "He has done everything well! He makes the deaf hear and the mute speak!"
(Mk 7:37)

24th SUNDAY IN ORDINARY TIME

Is 50:5–9
Jas 2:14–18
Mk 8:27–35

In today's readings, our Father asks us to take an
honest look at ourselves. Are we really trying to follow
Jesus? Or do we expend most of our time and energy per-
suing our own preconceived program in life?

The prophet Isaiah provides us with a beautiful
prayer which closely resembles a psalm in its literary style.
In even the most dificult situations in life, a true servant
of God continues to trust in God: "The Lord God is my
help, therefore I am not disgraced" (Is 50:7).

Jesus is the perfect realization of all the attempts by
faithful Jews to trust completely in God. Jesus' Father
asked him to trust in extremely trying circumstances: Although Jesus was perfectly innocent of all wrongdoings,
he was destined to be violently treated and executed. In
the gospel passage, Peter is correct in his expression of
faith: "You are the Messiah!" (Mk 8:29) Jesus is the
Messiah, the one who would pour out God's Spirit in our
world. But Jesus also knew that he was the suffering
Messiah. Peter objects because he cannot stand to see Jesus
rejected, mistreated and murdered. "Peter took Jesus
aside and began to reprimand him" (Mk 8:32). Jesus
answers Peter with surprising intensity: "Get out of my
sight, you Satan! You are not judging by God's standards
but by man's!" (Mk 8:33) Jesus then presents to Peter

and the other disciples the great paradox of Christian living: When we are willing to "lose" our lives for the sake of Jesus and the Good News of salvation in him, we will find a new way of life in Jesus! (Mk 8:35, 36)

James tells us in the second reading that we cannot claim to believe deeply in Jesus if we avoid being "inconvenienced" by the suffering of our brothers and sisters. The disturbing presence of people in need is a constant reminder to us that being a Christian is not a merely theoretical matter: "Faith that does nothing in practice. . . . is thoroughly lifeless" (Jas 2:17).

Our Messiah, who has died and is risen, is with us as we celebrate today's Eucharist. Because we are so reluctant to be the trusting people our Father wishes us to be, Jesus sends his Spirit into our hearts to overcome our stubbornness: "Brothers, what good is it to profess faith without practicing it?" (Jas 2:14) Encouraged by the Spirit of Jesus, we make the effort to "let go" of our own carefully planned agenda and seek new life in Jesus: "Whoever loses his life for my sake . . . will preserve it" (Mk 8:35).

25th SUNDAY IN ORDINARY TIME

Wis 2:12, 17–20
Jas 3:16 – 4:3
Mk 9:30–37

In the last several years, we have grown in our awareness of the meaning of sin in our lives. This change in our thinking is due mainly to the rediscovery of what the Bible tells us about sin. In the Bible, sin is never regarded as a mere infraction of a law. Sin is usually described in the context of important personal relationships: our relationship with God and our relationship with each other.

Our growing awareness of sin has been quite challenging to us. At times, it is an extremely painful process to build relationships and to pursue reconciliation when relationships have been weakened through sin. To make matters worse, we are so accustomed to excusing our failures to relate lovingly toward God and toward others that we are reluctant to admit the very existence of sin in our lives. Even the mention of the word "sin" bothers us. We feel more comfortable with milder terminology: shortcoming, fault, "hang-up." In today's readings, God asks us to be honest with ourselves. He asks us to recognize that we are sinners and that we need the Spirit of his Son in order to find true peace in our lives.

In the Old Testament reading, "the wicked" decide to plot against a person whose goodness irritates them. The conspirators boldly challenge God to intervene in order to demonstrate the innocence of their victim: "Let us find out what will happen to him. . . . God will defend him and deliver him from the hands of his foes" (Wis 2:17, 18). This passage reminds us of how the enemies of Jesus plotted to kill him. Indeed God did take care of Jesus, the Just One. Jesus' complete acceptance of the unjust circumstances surrounding his suffering and death was rewarded when the Father raised Jesus from the dead.

In today's gospel, Jesus speaks to his disciples about the stark realities of his suffering, death and rising. The disciples are shocked into silence, too frightened to ask Jesus what he meant by this unusual prediction. But soon they distract themselves in a heated argument "about who was the most important" (Mk 9:34). Jesus tells his followers that they will never be content in seeking positions of status. They will find true peace of mind only in following his own humble example. Jesus encourages them to serve others, especially people who are very persistent in their demands, for example, "a little child" (Mk 9:36, 37).

In our second reading, James points out the difference between authentic Christians, who act with "wisdom from above" (Jas 3:17), and people who pretend to be Christians. James criticizes this latter group who by their insidious rivalry are causing nothing but dissension in the Christian community. Harmony, James tells us, comes into our lives only through Jesus, whose dying and rising have brought lasting peace into our world: "The harvest of justice is sown in peace for those who cultivate peace" (Jas 3:18).

In today's readings, our Father invites us to recognize that Jesus is the only source of true peace and reconciliation in our lives. Our risen Brother is with us in our Eucharistic celebration. He comes to share his Spirit of peace with us. We pray the Eucharist, admitting our sinful tendencies and longing to experience within our community the peace which only the Spirit of Jesus can bring us.

26th SUNDAY IN ORDINARY TIME

Nm 11:25–29
Jas 5:1–6
Mk 9:38–43, 45, 47,48

Whenever we become preoccupied with comparing ourselves with others in our Christian community, we usually end up with feelings of bitterness and jealousy. In today's Liturgy of the Word, God asks us to stop comparing ourselves with others and to begin supporting each other in our decisions to believe in Jesus.

In the reading from Numbers, God sends the Holy Spirit on Moses while speaking to Moses. In turn, Moses bestows the gift of God's Spirit on other Israelites. Joshua becomes worried and reports to Moses that too many Israelites are giving manifestations of the Spirit. But Moses' reaction contains no jealousy: "Would that the Lord might bestow his Spirit on all!" (Nm 11:29)

Through Jesus the fulness of God's Spirit is poured out into our world. Whenever Jesus taught, he bestowed his Spirit on his listeners. If people were open to Jesus' gift of the Spirit, they accepted Jesus as their Savior and Messiah. In today's gospel, John becomes envious because a man who was not a recognized follower of Jesus was "using Jesus' name" (Mk 9:38). What John means is that the man was acting in the Spirit of Jesus. Our Lord assures John: "Anyone who is not against us is with us"

(Mk 9:40). A few verses beyond the conclusion of today's gospel, Jesus urges his disciples to avoid all jealousy and contention: "Be at peace with one another" (Mk 9:50).

At first glance, the passage from James' letter seems extremely harsh. But again we have to remind ourselves that James is writing to Christians. In today's passage, he warns the rich not to be absorbed with accumulating wealth by cheating the people who work for them: "See what you have stored up for yourselves against the last days. . . . The cries of the harvesters have reached the ears of the Lord" (Jas 5:3, 4). In the last analysis, wealth is unimportant. Only one thing really matters for us who are Christians—that we continue to seek salvation in Jesus. Jesus gives this same advice to his disciples: "If your hand is your difficulty. . . . If your foot is your undoing. . . . If your eye is your downfall. . . ." (Mk 9:43, 44, 45). Absolutely nothing should stand in the way of our making the decision to accept Jesus as our Savior.

Our risen Savior, filled with the Holy Spirit, comes among us today in our Eucharistic celebration. The Spirit helps us see what we must sacrifice to remain faithful to our Lord. Each of us is called upon to make uniquely personal sacrifices to be believers in Jesus. But we have to guard against the subtle temptations of jealousy. Jealousy among us is a certain sign that we are not entirely open to the Spirit. Jesus offers us his Spirit today to move us to give generous support to each other in the difficult decisions we make to accept Jesus as our Savior.

27th SUNDAY IN ORDINARY TIME

Gn 2:18–24
Heb 2:9–11
Mk 10:2–16 (Long Form),
or Mk 10:2–12 (Short Form)

For seven Sundays, beginning today, our second reading is selected from Paul's letter to Jewish Christians. In this Sunday's readings, we first proclaim how God created our first parents, Adam and Eve. Then we proclaim the Good News of God's New Creation of our human family through Jesus.

"God, for whom and through whom all things exist," (Heb 2:10), completes his first creation by calling Adam and Eve to marriage, the deepest, most rewarding of all human love relationships. Adam, no longer alone, is enthusiastic in praising God for his new companion: " 'This one, at last, is bone of my bones and flesh of my flesh'. . . . That is why a man leaves his father and mother and clings to his wife, and the two become one body" (Gn 2:23, 24). In the gospel, Jesus quotes this same passage from Genesis and emphasizes that marriage is a most serious relationship in which husband and wife make a sacred lifelong commitment to love each other (Mk 10:6–9).

By disobeying God, Adam and Eve brought unhappiness and disorder into the world. The tragedy of original sin might well have been the final chapter in human history. But God our loving Father had another plan. He promised to send a Savior to rescue us from sin. When Jesus came, he experienced the fulness of our human life, with all its joys and struggles. Finally, he suffered and died in order to transform us into God's sons and daughters (Heb 2:10). "He who consecrates and those who are consecrated have one and the same Father. Therefore he is not ashamed to call (us) brothers" (Heb 2:11). Since we "are men of blood and flesh, Jesus likewise had a full share in ours [in our human experience], that through his death he might rob the devil, the prince of death, of his power, and free those who through fear of death had become slaves their whole life long" (Heb 2:14–15).

Through Jesus' life, death and Resurrection, a New Creation takes place in the world. In baptism, we are recreated as members of God's family. Jesus shared the gift of his risen life with us. Our mysterious union with Jesus through grace can be compared to the love relationship between husband and wife. (See the 21st Sunday in Ordinary Time.) God's creative love has no limits! This is the wonderful message that we proclaim to the people who have become our brothers and sisters by sharing in the Easter mystery of Jesus.

As Christians, we celebrate Sunday as the Eighth Day of creation, the first day of God's New Creation in Jesus. Jesus our Brother, who died and was raised for us on Easter Sunday, joins us today in our Eucharistic celebration. He comes filling our hearts with his life-giving Spirit. Because the Spirit of Jesus lives in us, we are united to our risen Savior and to each other in a transformed human family. Jesus leads all of us in expressing our deep gratitude to our Father in our Eucharistic prayer: "You did not receive a spirit of slavery leading you back into fear, but a spirit of adoption through which we cry out, 'Abba! . . . Father!'" (Rom 8:15)

28th SUNDAY IN ORDINARY TIME

Wis 7:7–11
Heb 4:12,13
Mk 10:17–30 (Long Form),
or Mk 10:17–27 (Short Form)

Each Sunday we have an important responsibility as ministers of God's Word. Today, through us, God proclaims an important message to his people: "God's Word is living and effective, sharper than any two-edged sword. It penetrates . . . it judges the reflections and thoughts of the heart" (Heb 4:12).

For centuries before the coming of Jesus, people struggled to gain insight into the meaning of human life and asked profound questions about life beyond death. Gradually, throughout Salvation History and finally in Jesus, God revealed the complete meaning of our human experience. "In this, the final age, he has spoken to us through his Son" (Heb 1:2). Our loving Father invites us to believe in Jesus and to seek eternal salvation in him.

In today's gospel, Mark tells us that a man came running up to Jesus and asked him: "What must I do to share in everlasting life?'" (Mk 10:17) "Jesus looked at him with love" (Mk 10:21) and extended a very personal in-

vitation to the man: "Go and sell what you have. . . .
After that come and follow me" (Mk 10:21). There is
absolutely no other way to reach lasting life with God
except through Jesus, (*See* Jn 14:5.) Our Lord then turns
to his disciples and challenges them to re-examine their
own material and spiritual values: "How hard it is for
the rich to enter the Kingdom of God!" (Mk 10:23, 25)
The followers of Jesus are bewildered and "could only
marvel at his words" (Mk 10:24).

In our first reading, God tells us that he bestows
his wisdom only on people who sincerely seek more than
this life can ever give: "I pleaded and the Spirit of Wisdom came to me. I . . . deemed riches nothing in compari-
son with her. . . . Beyond health and comeliness I loved
her" (Wis 7:7, 8, 10).

Writing to the Jewish Christians, Paul asks them always to be open to God's Word: "Encourage one another
daily while it is still 'today,' so that no one grows hardened
by the deceit of sin" (Heb 3:13). Paul reminds these
early Christians of the disobedience of our Hebrew forefathers: "The word which they heard did not profit them,
for they did not receive it in faith" (Heb 4:2).

God speaks to our brothers and sisters through us. As
we proclaim the Scriptures, the risen Jesus, God's Word
in person, comes among us. Our Father invites us to respond to his Word by praying the Eucharist with a deeper
conviction that Jesus is our Savior. How shall we fare
today under the scrutiny of God's Word, which is "sharper
than any two-edged sword"? "Today, if you should hear
his voice, harden not your hearts as at the revolt!" (Heb
3:7, 8; Ps 95:7–9)

29th SUNDAY
IN ORDINARY TIME

Is 53:10,11
Heb 4:14–16
Mk 10:35–45

In selecting the readings for today's liturgy, the Church gives us a strong reminder. On each and every Sunday of the year, we celebrate the Easter mystery of Jesus. This is surely our reason for celebrating the Eucharist on this October Sunday, the 29th Sunday in Ordinary Time. In our three Scripture readings, God our Father invites us to share more deeply in Jesus' dying and rising. In fact, today's Eucharist might appropriately be called a Holy Week celebration in miniature.

The first two readings are shortened forms of the first two readings for Good Friday: "Through his suffering, my servant shall justify many, and their guilt he shall bear" (Is 53:11). "We have a great high priest who has passed through the heavens, Jesus, the Son of God. . . . So let us confidently approach the throne of grace to receive mercy and favor and to find help in time of need" (Heb 4:16, 16).

Our gospel reading closely parallels the gospel for the Evening Mass of Holy Thursday. Mk 10:35–45 is a beautiful description of Jesus' eagerness to serve others. Our Lord showed this same willingness to serve in such an impressive manner when he washed the feet of his disciples in the upper room. In today's gospel, Jesus clearly tells his disciples the meaning of true greatness: "You know how among the Gentiles . . . their great ones make their importance felt. It cannot be that way with you. . . . whoever wants to be first among you must serve the needs of all" (Mk 10:42, 43, 44).

Jesus "was tempted in every way that we are, yet never sinned" (Heb 4:15). Jesus not only avoided obvious temptations. He also refused to be trapped by the most subtle of all human temptations: manipulating and controlling others to serve his own needs. "The Son of Man has not come to be served but to serve—to give his life in ransom for the many" (Mk 10:45; Is 53:11).

Today when we gather for our Eucharistic meal, our risen Brother will be among us. He calls us to celebrate the Eucharist as his authentic community of believers, people who are willing to serve each other's needs and to accept loving service from each other. "I give you a new commandment. Love one another. Such as my love has been for you, so must your love be for each other. This is how all will know you for my disciples: your love for one another" (Jn 13:34, 35).

30th SUNDAY IN ORDINARY TIME

Jer 31:7–9
Heb 5:1–6
Mk 10:46–52

Today's readings give us an opportunity for serious self-examination. How open are we to receive the life which our Father gives us in his risen Son?

As the chosen people in the Old Testament awaited Christ's coming, many of them rejected their Sinai relationship with God and no longer looked to God for deliverance. In today's first reading, the prophet Jeremiah describes a faithful few, "the remnant of Israel," who refused to waver in their trust in God (Jer 31:7). Despite repeated personal and national setbacks and hardships, the remnant held fast to their belief in God. They knew that God had not deserted his people and that he would surely be faithful to his promise to send them a Savior.

In today's gospel, Bartimaeus clearly displays the hopeful attitude of the remnant of Israel: "On hearing that it was Jesus of Nazareth, he began to call out, 'Jesus, Son of David, have pity on me!' Many people were scolding him to make him quiet, but he shouted all the louder, 'Son of David, have pity on me!' " (Mk 10:47, 48) Bartimaeus is blind and poor, but he does not give up hope in God. With a determined faith, he seeks and finds God's healing power in Jesus. Like any of us who decide to turn to Jesus for salvation, Bartimaeus is not disappointed: "Jesus said . . . 'Be on your way. Your faith has healed you!' " (Mk 10:52)

The attitude of the faithful Israelite is fully revealed and exemplified in Jesus. Although he was God's Son from all eternity, Jesus willingly accepted the weakness of our human condition and looked to his Father for fulfilment of all his needs: "He emptied himself and took on the form of a slave, being born in the likeness of men. . . . He humbled himself, obediently accepting even death, death on a cross!" (Phil 2:7, 8) The dying Jesus embodied all the hopes and dreams of the faithful Jewish remnant. Because he poured himself out fully in loving obedience, "God highly exalted him and bestowed on him the name above every other name" (Phil 2:9). Jesus became our perfect high priest by offering himself totally to his Father. "Even Christ did not glorify himself with the office of high priest; he received it from the One who said to him, 'You are my son; today I have begotten you' " (Heb 5:5), Jesus, who was always God's Son, became in his Resurrection "the Son of God in power" (Rom 1:4).

Our risen high priest is with us today as we worship. He invites us to follow his example by entrusting all our needs to our Father. It is only when we discover our own emptiness that our loving Father can fill us with risen life in his Son.

31st SUNDAY IN ORDINARY TIME

Dt 6:2–6
Heb 7:23–28
Mk 12:28–34

In today's gospel, Jesus quotes the Old Testament and clearly spells out the two great commandments which he expects us to obey: "You shall love the Lord your God with all your heart. . . . You shall love your neighbor as yourself" (Mk 12:30, 31; Dt 6:4; Lev 19:18). This Sunday's Liturgy of the Word helps us to see how we can express our love for God and our love for each other in our Eucharistic celebration.

In our first reading, Moses challenges the Israelites to obey all of God's commandments. By obeying the commandments, the Israelites would demonstrate their willingness to be the people whom God had made his very own by delivering them from Egypt: "Hear, O Israel! The Lord is our God, the Lord alone! Therefore, you shall love the Lord your God, with all your heart" (Dt 6:4, 5).

In Paul's letter to the Jewish Christians, he contrasts the new covenant with the old. "Under the old covenant there were many priests" (Heb 7:23). But in Jesus, we have both the perfect priest and the perfect offering— Jesus' gift of himself! In his love-filled death, Jesus fulfilled completely the two great commandments. He lovingly offered himself "once for all" to his Father on our behalf. Jesus died but once, but he is a priest forever. As risen Savior, he continues to give himself completely to his Father and to us: "He is always able to save those who approach God through him, since he forever lives to make intercession for them" (Heb 7:25).

The risen Jesus, our eternal high priest, is the source of all our efforts to express love for God and for each other. He is with us once again as we share our Eucharistic meal today. Jesus invites us to join him in his perfect act of self-giving through which we are reconciled to God and to each other.

32nd SUNDAY IN ORDINARY TIME

1 Kgs 17:10–16
Heb 9:24–28
Mk 12:38–44

The theme of today's readings is generosity. In the first reading, the widow accepted God's word spoken to her through the prophet Elijah. God rewarded her faith and her generosity by providing her with a miraculous supply of flour and oil.

In the gospel, Jesus calls to the attention of his disciples the generous sacrifice of the poor widow: She "contributed more than all the others who donated to the treasury. . . . She gave from her want, all that she had to live on" (Mk 12:43, 44).

In suffering and dying, Jesus gave us the greatest manifestation of love. The Father rewarded the generosity of his Son by raising him from the dead: "God highly exalted him and bestowed on him the name above every other name" (Phil 2:9). In our second reading, Paul tells us how the risen Jesus continues to express his unique act of generosity before the Father: Jesus "entered heaven itself that he might appear before God now on our behalf" (Heb 9:24).

This same risen Jesus is with us as we gather to celebrate the Eucharist today. Our efforts to express our generosity in our Eucharistic action will be successful, because we offer ourselves in a way that is entirely pleasing to our Father. We offer ourselves through Jesus, with Jesus, and in Jesus!

33rd SUNDAY IN ORDINARY TIME

Dn 12:1–3
Heb 10:11–14, 18
Mk 13:24–32

On this next to the last Sunday of the year, we celebrate a theme of judgment. In the Bible, God tells us that Jesus, our risen Brother, is central in the divine plan to judge us: "Jesus offered one sacrifice for sins and took his seat forever at the right hand of God; now he waits until his enemies are placed beneath his feet. By one offering he has forever perfected those who are being sanctified" (Heb 10:12–14).

In today's gospel, Jesus uses a special kind of symbolic language. It is the same language that we find in our reading from the prophet Daniel. Jesus' followers immediately recognize that he is speaking about God's judgment in the world. In the Bible, judgment has two characteristics: 1) God intervenes in human history; 2) God then judges people according to their acceptance or rejection of what God is doing. In speaking about judgment in today's gospel, Jesus is actually inviting us to choose him as our Savior. Our judgment takes place on the basis of whether or not we accept Jesus, who is God's full offer of salvation to us.

All of us will inevitably have to face death, that important moment when God will judge our entire life. But our judgment is not completely an event in the future. As we celebrate our Eucharistic today, the risen Jesus is with us. We are being judged today on our willingness to seek lasting life in Jesus, who is present and active among us. "Let us hold unswervingly to our profession which gives us hope, for he who made the promise deserves our trust" (Heb 10:23).

34th SUNDAY IN ORDINARY TIME

Dn 7:13–14
Rv 1:5–8
Jn 18:33–37

Today we conclude the "Cycle B" liturgical year with a celebration of the feast of Christ our King. Jesus is a unique kind of king, the "ruler of the kings of the earth" (Rv 1:5). He is king forever: "His dominion is an everlasting dominion that shall not be taken away, his kingship shall not be destroyed" (Dn 7:14). Mysteriously, Jesus' Kingdom "does not belong to this world" (Jn 18:36). Today's readings enlighten us and direct our attention to Jesus our King, who is actively present among us in our Eucharistic celebration.

In the gosple, Jesus undergoes questioning by Pilate: "Are you the king of the Jews?" (Jn 18:36) Jesus replies by telling Pilate about his kingship: "The reason I was born . . . is to testify to the truth. Anyone committed to the truth hears my voice" (Jn 18:37). Hearing Jesus'

voice means believing in him and in his power to transform us.

In other passages in John's gospel, Jesus describes the
kind of pervading influence he wishes to exercise in our
lives: "Jesus said to those Jews who believed in him:
'If you live according to my teaching, you are truly my
disciples; then you will know the truth and the truth will
set you free" (Jn 8:21, 32). Jesus, "the first-born from
the dead" (Rv 1:5), offered himself so that we might be
transformed in him: "I consecrate myself for their sakes
now, that they may be consecrated in truth. . . . Just
Father. . . . to them I have revealed your name, and I
will continue to reveal it so that your love for me may
live in them, and I may live in them" (Jn 17:19, 25, 26).
By dying and rising, Jesus exercises his kingship and control over our lives: "Now has judgment come upon this
world, now will this world's prince be driven out, and I—
once I am lifted up from earth—will draw all men to
myself" (Jn 12:31, 22).

Jesus is with us as we gather for today's Eucharist.
He invites us to open our hearts to him so that we can
be transformed by his saving love. In our Eucharistic
prayer, we praise our risen King in our midst: "To him
who loves us and freed us from our sins by his own blood,
who made us a royal nation of priests in the service of
his God and Father—to him be glory and power forever
and ever! Amen!" (Rv 1:5, 6)

OTHER MAJOR FEASTS

December 8
THE IMMACULATE CONCEPTION

Gn 3:9–15, 20
Eph 1:3–6, 11,12
Lk 1:26–38

Today we celebrate the feast of Mary's Immaculate Conception. We can best consider the privilege of the Immaculate Conception in the context of Adam's sin and salvation through Jesus: "Just as through one man's disobedience, all became sinners, so through one man's obedience all shall become just" (Rom 5:19).

As sons and daughters of Adam, we are born sinners. Today, we observe an exception to the phenomenon of original sin. God gave Mary a special gift, which we call her Immaculate Conception. Mary, the mother of Jesus, who is our Savior and her Savior, was preserved from all sin, Adam's sin as well as her own. Our loving Father predestined that Mary would be free from sin from the first moment of her existence. "Rejoice, O highly favored daughter! The Lord is with you" (Lk 1:28). The Immaculate Conception, however, does not mean that Mary did not need to be saved by Jesus.

Well before Mary was capable of making decisions, including her all important decision to accept salvation from God, she was given a share in God's life. Later, as Mary began to develop into adulthood and make decisions, she looked entirely to God for salvation. Like our own faith decision, Mary's most significant decision was to accept her Son as her Savior. Her decision deepened as Jesus' life unfolded, particularly in the events of the Easter mystery: the dying and rising of Jesus, and the risen Jesus sending his Spirit upon his community of believers, which included Mary. God gave Mary the insight to recognize that he loved her in a special way. Mary humbly accepted all of God's unique gifts to her: "I am the servant of the Lord. Let it be done to me as you say" (Lk 1:38). "God who is mighty has done great things for me" (Lk 1:49).

Today we honor Mary, our sister, specially chosen by

God to be the Mother of Jesus. As we celebrate the Eucharist, our risen brother is here among us. We express our belief that Jesus died and was raised by God to save all of us: "Through one man's obedience all shall become just" (Rom 5:19). Praying with Jesus, who is present among us, we praise our Father for Mary's Immaculate Conception and the other gifts which God has bestowed on her: "Praised be the God and Father of our Lord Jesus Christ, who has bestowed on us in Christ every spiritual blessing in the heavens" (Eph 1:3).

January 1
World Day of
PRAYER FOR PEACE

*Is 9:1–6
Eph 4:30 – 5:2
Mt 5:20–24

Today we proclaim Scripture passages which give us an appropriate setting for today's theme: World Day of Prayer for Peace.

To be honest about it, all of us experience a difficulty in being peaceful. And so, the peace we pray for today is not "somebody else's problem." The most effective way that we can join our hearts in a World Day of Prayer for Peace is by trying to be peaceful in our lives, in our relationships. But the peace we pray for is not reached entirely by our own efforts. The peace we seek is a gift from God: "Peace is my farewell to you, my peace is my gift to you" (Jn 14:27).

In the first reading, Isaiah gives a prophecy about the Messiah: "For a child is born to us, a Son is given us. . . . They name him . . . Prince of Peace. His dominion is vast and forever peaceful" (Is 9:5, 6).

Paul tells us in the second reading that we can "sadden the Holy Spirit" (Eph 4:30) whom the risen Jesus first gave us in baptism. We sadden the Spirit by our "bitterness . . . anger, harsh words, slander" (Eph 4:31). It is a never ending challenge for us to seek peace and reconciliation with those to whom we relate each and every day. Is there someone to whom we have failed to say, "I'm sorry" or "I forgive you"? Jesus tells us in the gospel that our reconciliation with God cannot occur without our openness toward each other: "Go first to be reconciled with your brother, and then come and offer your gift" (Mt 5:24).

We are gathered together for the Eucharist in which we express our intention to love as Jesus loved us (Eph 5:2; Jn 13:34). Jesus is with us today and sends his Spirit into our hearts to bring us peace. We pray the Eucharist, longing to experience within our hearts the peace which comes when we are truly reconciled to God and to each other.

The lectionary contains other readings which are optional for this day.

February 2
THE PRESENTATION
OF THE LORD

Mal 3:1–4
Heb 2:14–18
Lk 2:22–40 (Long Form),
or Lk 2:22–32 (Short Form)

Today we celebrate the feast of the Presentation of Jesus in the temple. It was an ancient Jewish custom to dedicate every first-born son to God and then to buy back (redeem) that son from God by offering a gift in the temple. This custom reminded the Jews of how God slew the first-born sons of the Egyptians and delivered his own people from Egypt: "Every first-born son you must redeem. If your son should ask you later on, 'What does this mean?' you shall tell him, 'With a strong hand the LORD brought us out of Egypt, that place of slavery'" (Ex 13:13, 14).

It was a special day in the history of Israel and the world when Mary and Joseph brought their son to the temple to be consecrated to God. Jesus was destined to be the Messiah whose sacrifice would be completely ac-

ceptable to God (Mal 3:1–4). Through his dying and
rising, Jesus delivered from sinful bondage God's new
people (Lk 2:38). To be freed from our sins, we have
to recognize the importance of Jesus' decision to give of
himself fully on the cross. In his love-filled death, Jesus
counteracted Adam's tragic decision. Adam had tried to
find a full answer to human life within himself, apart
from his love relationship with God. Adam failed. Without Jesus, we fail too. Without our Savior, we live and
die as prisoners of our own fears (Heb 2:14, 15). But
now we have the opportunity to become a liberated people who find favor with God—if we are willing to stake
our lives on the dying and rising of Jesus.

In today's gospel, our Lord entered the temple to
be consecrated to God. Jesus once again enters a temple
today as he becomes present in us, his people, gathered
for worship. We are the Lord's living temple, whether
we celebrate the Eucharist in a church, or at home, or in
a storefront: "You . . . are living stones, built as an edi-
fice of spirit . . . offering spiritual sacrifices acceptable to
God through Jesus Christ" (I Pt 2:5). Our risen brother
is here. He is our "merciful and faithful high priest before God" (Heb 2:17), pleading with the Father on our
behalf. As we celebrate the Eucharist, we can "confidently
approach the throne of grace to receive mercy and favor
and to find help in time of need" (Heb 4:16).

March 19
ST. JOSEPH

2 Sm 7:4,5, 12–14, 16
Rom 4:13, 16–18, 22
*Mt 1:16, 18–21, 24

Today we celebrate the feast of St. Joseph. We learn
very little from the Bible about the man who was chosen
by God to be the foster father of Jesus. In fact, in today's
three readings, only the gospel mentions Joseph by name.

It is unfortunate that religious art has frequently
depicted Joseph with a lily in his hand—hardly a symbol

of masculine strength. And yet, Joseph must have been a strong man because, in a unique way, he influenced the development of the child Jesus. We know that Jesus' real father was God from all eternity. But Jesus learned to relate to Joseph as his father and experienced in his relationship with Joseph the warmth and love of a concerned father for his son.

Today's readings have been selected to help us reflect on Joseph, the man of faith: "When Joseph awoke he did as the angel of the Lord had directed him" (Mt 1:24). Like Abraham, Joseph's faith centered around the mysterious circumstances of the birth of a child. "Fully persuaded that God could do whatever he had promised" (Rom 4:21), Joseph accepted God's word when God told him that the Messiah, the promised descendent of David (2 Sm 7:12, 13, 16), was Mary's child: "She is to have a son and you are to name him Jesus because he will save his people from their sins" (Mt 1:21).

Jesus, our risen Savior, the foster son of Joseph, is here with us as we celebrate the Eucharist. Our worship today can be the expression of our faith in Jesus, who lived, died and was raised from the dead to fulfill Old Testament prophecies about the Savior of the world.

Lk 2:41–51 is an optional gospel reading.

March 25
ANNUNCIATION
OF CHRIST

Is 7:10–14
Heb 10:4–10
Lk 1:26–38

Today is our celebration of the feast of the Annunciation, the angel Gabriel's announcement to Mary that she was to be the mother of Jesus. In the readings, we proclaim the awesome mystery of the Incarnation: Jesus, God's Son from all eternity, became our human brother, the son of a young Jewish girl.

Ahaz, King of Israel, refused to place his trust in God (Is 7:12). Nonetheless, God remains faithful to his people by promising a child, Immanuel (God-with-us) to be born of a young girl (Is 7:14).

The "remnant of Israel" was a group of Jews who trusted that God would deliver his people through the promised Messiah (Zep 3:12). In today's gospel, Mary represents all the faithful remnant of Israel. The angel greets her: "Rejoice, O highly favored daughter!" (Lk 1:28) Mary does not pretend to understand all that God is saying to her (Lk 1:34), but she is filled with faith and trust in God: "Let it be done to me as you say." (Lk 1:38)

Jesus, our brother, fully shared our human experience in order to give us the opportunity to share his experience of relating to God as his Father (Mt 11:25–27). His entire life was a giving of himself to the Father: "I have come to do your will" (Heb 10:9). Through Jesus' sacrifice offered (his dying) and accepted (the Father raising Jesus from the dead), we now can become adopted sons and daughters of God: "We have been sanctified through the offering of the body of Jesus Christ once for all" (Heb 10:10). Through the dying and rising of Jesus, we are acceptable to our Father.

Today we proclaim to our brothers and sisters the mystery of the Incarnation, "God-with-us." The Incarnation is not an event buried in past history. As we celebrate the Eucharist, our risen brother is acting among us. Mary's son, our Immanuel, is here!

SUNDAY AFTER PENTECOST
TRINITY SUNDAY

Dt 4:32–34, 39,40
Rom 8:14–17
Mt 28:16–20

Today we celebrate Trinity Sunday. The Scripture readings throughout the seasons of Lent and Easter have frequently called our attention to the unique love relationship which we have with each of the three Divine Persons: God our Father expresses his saving love toward us in his Son. Jesus saves us through his death and Resurrection, the pivotal events in salvation history. Now as risen Lord, Jesus sends the Spirit of love into our hearts. United to Jesus in the Spirit, we are transformed into God's responsive sons and daughters: "All who are led by the Spirit of God are sons of God" (Rom: 8:14).

It is impossible for us to attempt to describe the mystery of our salvation without also considering the mystery of the Blessed Trinity. As Christians, we confess our belief that in one God there are three Divine Persons: Father, Son and Holy Spirit. But does our belief in the Trinity make any real impact on the way we live and worship?

Our appreciation of the mystery of the Triune God can begin with our prayerful meditation on God's interaction with the Israelites as described in the books of the Old Testament. God revealed himself to the Israelites as a God who was continually seeking to initiate a profound love relationship with his people. Time and time again, God invited the Israelites to encounter him by recalling to them the events surrounding the Sinai covenant, God's great overture of love for his people. In today's first reading, Moses is trying to remind the Israelites of their unusual relationship with God: "Did anything so great ever happen before? Was it ever heard of? Did a people ever hear the voice of God . . . as you did and live?" (Dt 4:32, 33) Because God was so generous in his love, he demanded a total, wholehearted response from his people: "You must now know, and fix in your heart, that the Lord is God . . . and that there is no other" (Dt 4:39).

When Jesus came, he revealed to us the fatherhood of God and the full mystery of the Trinity. "No one has ever seen God. It is God the only Son, ever at the Father's side, who has revealed him" (Jn 1:18). In everything Jesus said and did, he revealed his loving Father. Jesus also shared with us his unique, intense awareness of being

the Beloved of his Father. The Holy Spirit, the Third
Person of the Trinity, was also active throughout the life
of Jesus, because the Spirit is the personal bond of love
between Jesus and his Father.

In today's gospel, Jesus commanded the Apostles:
"Go . . . baptize . . . in the name of the Father, and of the
Son, and of the Holy Spirit" (Mt 28:19). It was at our
baptism when our heavenly Father first called us to share
in the very life of the Trinity. In the letter to the Romans,
Paul tells us that in baptism we were united to Jesus
in his dying and rising: "You must consider yourselves
dead to sin but alive for God in Christ Jesus" (Rom 6:11).
"Being alive for God in Christ Jesus" means that God's
Spirit lives in us: "The love of God has been poured out
in our hearts through the Holy Spirit who has been given
to us" (Rom 5:5).

Today, the feast of the Trinity, we recommit ourselves as baptized Christians who relate lovingly to God
the Father, Son and Holy Spirit. We join with our brothers
and sisters to thank our Father for saving us. Salvation
is offered to us by our loving Father, through Jesus, who
gives us the Spirit. Moved by the Spirit, we respond to
our Father through Jesus. These "upward and downward
movements" really happen to us as we celebrate today's
Eucharist: Our Father once again sends his Son among
us. The risen Jesus, in our midst, pours the Holy Spirit
into our hearts so that we can fearlessly and lovingly respond to our Father in our Eucharistic prayer: "All who
are led by the Spirit of God are sons of God. You did not
receive a spirit of slavery, leading you back into fear, but
a spirit of adoption through which we cry out, 'Abba' . . .
Father' " (Rom 8:14–15).

BODY AND BLOOD OF CHRIST
CORPUS CHRISTI

Ex 24:3–8
Heb 9:11–15
Mk 14:12–16, 22–26

Today we have the opportunity to deepen our Eucharistic devotion. The three readings for this feast emphasize the biblical symbolism of blood. For the Jews and for Jesus, blood signified life. The ritual of sprinkling blood on two individuals or on two groups of people signified the forming of a living, lasting relationship of love and friendship between them. This is what convenant means in the Bible.

The first reading describes a key event in the Old Testament: the solemn enacting of the Sinai convenant between God and Israel. God had delivered the Israelites from Egypt and led them into the desert. Then God spoke to his people through Moses and asked them for their complete response of love. The Israelites gave their assent: "We will do everything that the Lord has told us" (Ex 24:3). To ratify this unique love relationship between God and his people, Moses performed a familiar ritual. He sprinkled blood on the altar, which represented God, and on the people. Page after page in the Old Testament, however, describes how the Israelites repeatedly violated the Sinai covenant. But God never wavered in his commitment to his people. Finally, God fully manifested his love for us by sending his Son to live among us.

The gospel reading sets the scene for the Lord's Supper, which took place "on the first day of Unleavened Bread, when it was customary to sacrifice the paschal lamb" (Mk 14:12). With his attention focused on his dying and rising, Jesus celebrates the Eucharist to reconcile us with his Father. In the blood of Jesus, our loving Father seals and ratifies his final and lasting covenant with us. Our covenant relationship with God no longer depends in any way on bloody animal sacrifices (Heb 9:13, 14). We are saved from our sins and brought into a new relationship with God through the perfect sacrifice of love expressed by Jesus on the cross (Heb 9:15).

Today at our Eucharist, Jesus renews our covenant with the Father. Once again, Jesus acts through the priest as he takes the cup into his hands and says: "This is the cup of my blood, the blood of the new and everlasting covenant" (from the Order of the Mass, ICEL). At the end of the great prayer of thanksgiving, we will hear the priest proclaim: "Through him, with him, in him, in the unity of the Holy Spirit, all honor and glory is yours, almighty Father, for ever and ever" (from the Order of the Mass, ICEL). With hearts filled with confidence and love, let us respond: "Amen!" "All that the Lord has said, we will heed and do!" (Ex 24:7)

June 24
THE BIRTH OF
JOHN THE BAPTIST

Is 49:1–6
Acts 13:22–26
Lk 1:57–66, 80

Today we celebrate the birthday of John the Baptist, the prophet chosen by God to announce the arrival of the Messiah. When John preached, he caused a great stir among the people because they had been without a prophet for many generations.

In the first reading, we learn what God expected from a prophet. As God's spokesman, he was to remind the Israelites of God's love for them and invite them to recommit themselves to God by renewing the Sinai covenant: "That Jacob may be brought back to him and Israel gathered to him" (Is 49:5). The salvation proclaimed by God's prophet was to be offered to both the Israelites and the entire world. God says to Isaiah: "I will make you a light to the nations, that my salvation may reach to the ends of the earth" (Is 49:6). God chose John to introduce Jesus to the world.

John was born six months before Jesus. Today's gospel message narrates the mysterious birth of the prophet:

"Who will this child be?" (Lk 1:66) In Acts, we are told that John became a true witness to Jesus. He always pointed toward Jesus in his preaching: "Look for the one who comes after me." (Acts 13:25; *also see* Mt 3:11.)

Today, Jesus, the Messiah announced by John the Baptist, is present among us. As we celebrate the Eucharist, we can thank God for the privilege of announcing to our brothers and sisters that Jesus, our Savior, has come to us!

June 29
PETER AND PAUL,
Apostles

Acts 12:1–11
2 Tm 4:6–8, 17–18
Mt 16:13–19

Today we celebrate the feastday of two great men, Peter and Paul. They were apostles, men sent by God to announce the Good News of salvation in Jesus. To accomplish their mission, Peter and Paul were willing to make any sacrifice, even to the extent of giving their very lives, as Jesus did, to announce to people God's offer of salvation in Jesus.

In the first two readings, each apostle gives a beautiful, stirring testimony of how God rescued him from the hands of his enemies. In the gospel, Jesus promises to Peter that the Church of Jesus would never be destroyed. With God's help, the Church will continue, despite human failings, under the guidance of Peter and the apostles and their successors. The Church of Jesus is built on God's power and revelation, not on human strength and insight: "Blest are you, Simon son of Jonah! No mere man has revealed this to you, but my heavenly Father" (Mt 16:17).

Jesus is the founder of the Church in two ways. First, Jesus began the Church 2,000 years ago. Jesus is also founder in the sense that he continues to send his Spirit on the Church throughout history and at this very moment in time. As Peter and Paul preached salvation in Jesus, they were very aware of this continuing, dynamic presence of the risen Jesus in their midst.

As readers, we proclaim to our brothers and sisters that the same risen Jesus is present among us as we celebrate the Eucharist today. We rejoice because Jesus continues to act in the Church to give needed strength and lasting life to us who accept him as our Savior. We greet our Lord here in our midst: "You are the Messiah . . . the Son of the living God!" (Mt 16:16).

August 6
THE TRANSFIGURATION
OF OUR LORD

Dn 7:9,10, 13,14
2 Pt 1:16–19
Mk 9:2–10

Today we celebrate our Lord's Transfiguration, which was a preview of his Resurrection. The Transfiguration was one of the most mysterious events in the life of Jesus.

In the second reading, Peter describes Jesus' Transfiguration as "the coming in power of our Lord Jesus Christ" (2 Pt 1:16). Peter, one of the three eyewitnesses of what happened to Jesus on the mountain, searches for words to describe the unusual event: Jesus "received glory and praise from God the Father when that unique declaration came to him out of the majestic splendor: 'This is my beloved Son, on whom my favor rests'" (2 Pt 1:17). The Father manifests for a moment the complete splendor of Jesus who, as risen Lord, will fully reveal the life which he receives from his Father.

As we celebrate the Eucharist today, our risen Lord is here. He is the same Jesus who was once transfigured before Peter, James, and John. Today, our Father again praises his Son and invites us to stake our lives on Jesus: "This is my Son, my Beloved. Listen to him" (Mk 9:7). In our celebration, we express our belief that Jesus is here to share his risen life with us. We also express our hope that we will one day experience fully our life in Jesus, when he comes in glory on the last day to complete our transformation in him (Dn 7:13, 14).

August 15
THE ASSUMPTION
OF THE BLESSED VIRGIN

Rv 11:19, 12:1–6, 10
1 Cor 15:20–26
Lk 1:39–56

Today in our liturgy, we express our belief that God took Mary, body and soul, into heaven. After Mary died, God granted her the unique privilege of enjoying the fulness of life in Jesus. She now enjoys the complete experience of being alive in her risen Son.

In today's readings, we proclaim Mary as the mother of Jesus, her Savior and ours. The first reading symbolically describes the woman who gives birth to "a boy destined to shepherd all the nations" (Rv 12:5).

In Paul's first letter to the Corinthians, he compares our two brothers, Adam and Jesus. These two men have had such far-reaching effects on us: "Death came through a man; hence the resurrection of the dead comes through a man also. Just as in Adam all die, so in Christ all will come to life again" (1 Cor 15:21–22). Mary's Assumption is her bodily resurrection in Jesus. Body and soul, that is, as a complete human person, Mary fully experiences risen life in her Son.

In today's gospel, Elizabeth, Mary's cousin, is "filled with the Holy Spirit" (Lk 1:41), and begins to praise Mary: "Blest are you among women. . . . Blest is she who trusted that the Lord's words to her would be fulfilled" (Lk 1:42, 45). But Mary directs her own attention to God to praise him for her gifts: "My being proclaims the greatness of the Lord. . ." (Lk 1:46). Mary's gifts and privileges are from God.

As we gather to celebrate the Eucharist today, our

risen Savior is here. The life he now shares with us will
be fully realized in us at the general resurrection on the
last day. That is what we anticipate as we celebrate Mary's
Assumption. What has already happened to Mary will
one day happen to us. In heaven, we shall enjoy, in soul
and body, the life of Jesus. We have reason to be hopeful
that God will also grant us the gift of life beyond death,
because Mary's Son, our risen brother, is present among
us. In him, "all will come to life again" (1 Cor 15:22).

September 14
THE EXULTATION
OF THE HOLY CROSS

Nm 21:4–9
Phil 2:6–11
Jn 3:13–17

Good Friday and today's feast, The Exultation of
the Holy Cross, are the two days in the liturgical year when
we praise God in a special manner for the cross of Jesus.
On Good Friday, of course, our celebration is restrained.
Today, however, we express our joy openly and enthusiastically, because "God so loved the world that he gave
his only Son" (Jn 3:16). God's great love for us invites
us to respond. We can be saved by deciding to believe
in the love-filled death of Jesus on the cross.
The Old Testament reading concerns an event in
the lives of the Israelites as they journeyed through the
desert. God had already delivered the Israelites from
Egypt and had selected them as his very own people. But
they grew tired and refused to respond with love and
confidence to God: "Why have you brought us up from
Egypt to die in this desert, where there is no food or
water?" (Nm 21:5). Then God punished his people for
their lack of confidence in him. But being a God of love
and forgiveness, he gave them another chance. The people
who decided to trust in God by following Moses' instruc-
tions recovered from the fatal snake bite (Nm 21:8, 9).
Without Jesus, we inevitably face everlasting death.

But Jesus was first lifted up on the cross and then lifted up by his Father in the loving embrace which is Jesus' Resurrection. When we "look on" the cross of Jesus with love, when we decide to accept God's salvation for us in the dying and rising of Jesus, we are saved from lasting death: "That whoever believes in him may not die but may have eternal life" (Jn 3:16).

The second reading is Paul's hymn of praise for the entire life, death, and Resurrection of Jesus. Jesus, God's eternal Son, became one of us in a very unpretentious manner: not as risen Lord in glory, but as humble Servant (Phil 2:6, 7). With loving obedience, he chose to fulfill his Father's will by dying on a cross (Phil 2:8). Because of Jesus' complete emptying of himself in love, the Father raised him up and exalted him! (Phil 2:9) Then in our proclamation to our brothers and sisters, we join our voices: "Let every tongue proclaim, to the glory of God the Father: JESUS CHRIST IS LORD!" (Phil 2:11)

Today we proclaim Jesus, who saves us through his full expression of love on the cross and through his Resurrection. As readers, we openly and joyfully express our belief that Jesus has been lifted up by the Father and is now in our midst as our source of everlasting life. In the Eucharist, we respond to God's love for us in Jesus. We praise our Father by praying with an awareness that our life-giving Savior is present among us as we worship.

November 1
ALL SAINTS DAY

Rv 7:2–4, 9–14
1 Jn 3:1–3
Mt 5:1–12

Today we celebrate the feast day of all the saints, including all the people whose lives will never be closely scrutinized in the canonization process. The names of such saints will never appear on a Church calendar and are included in the group called "All Saints." In the first reading, John describes his vision of this saintly group: "I saw before me a huge crowd which no one could count from every nation and race, people and tongue" (Rv 7:9).

What all the saints have in common is that during their lifetime, they made the decision to accept Jesus as their Savior and they remained faithful, with God's help, to that decision. They now proclaim in heaven the decision which they made on earth: "Salvation is from our God, who is seated on the throne, and from the Lamb!" (Rv 7:10)

The saints were baptized in Jesus and had their sins forgiven. They were tried and tested, and they remained faithful to Jesus (Rv 7:14). John, an important author in the New Testament, never ceased to be astonished about God's love for us: "See what love the Father has bestowed on us in letting us be called children of God! Yet that is what we are" (1 Jn 3:1). "We are God's children now" (1 Jn 3:2). We are already God's children because we have been baptized in the risen Jesus and are now alive in him.

In the gospel, Jesus gives the beatitudes. Jesus is not speaking about eight or nine different groups of people, each with a different reward. He is using the Hebrew parallel style of expression to describe the same reward for the same attitude. That attitude, an openness to receive the gift of God's salvation in Jesus, is what makes ordinary people saints: "They cried out in a loud voice, 'Salvation is from our God, who is seated on the throne, and from the Lamb!'" (Rv 7:10)

No matter how aggressive we choose to be in our approach to other things, we can exercise only one option if we wish to be saved. We have to be willing to accept God's initiative: his offer of salvation to us in Jesus. So much of our aggressiveness may be able to be traced to our reluctance to make such a faith decision. Perhaps our inner restlessness is a sign that we are not "giving in" to God who alone can give us true inner peace.

Jesus, our Savior, is actively present as we worship today. By sending his Son to be with us, our Father is inviting us to make a firmer decision to accept Jesus as our Savior. This commitment prepares us to join our brothers and sisters in heaven. Jesus leads us in our Eucharistic celebration today. With all our brothers and sisters in heaven, we join our voices as we joyfully praise our Father: "Amen! Praise and glory, wisdom and thanksgiving and honor, power and might, to our God forever and ever. Amen!" (Rv 7:12)

November 2
ALL SOULS DAY

*Dn 12:1–3
Rom 6:3–11
Jn 5:24–29

Today, we celebrate the feast of the faithful departed, the people who have lived and died as true believers in Jesus, but who are not yet "in heaven" with God. As Catholics, we believe that there is a time of purgation for people who die "in the state of grace" (alive in the risen Lord), but who are not yet ready to experience the Beatific Vision. Seeing God "face to face" (1 Cor 13:12) means to experience fully our most important love relationship: the awareness of being loved by God in Jesus, along with our wholehearted response to God's love. All Souls Day is a special day of prayer for our departed brothers and sisters who are now being purified in their ability to love.

At the end of our lives, God will judge us on how we have used our ability to love. In today's readings, God speaks to us about judgment. Dn 12:1–3 is written in the symbolic biblical language which was used to describe judgment. In the Bible, judgment has two characteristics: 1) God intervenes in history; 2) God then judges people according to their acceptance or rejection of what God is doing. Jesus himself used this same symbolic language in Mt 24 when he explained God's last judgment in history: 1) In Jesus, God has intervened in our lives in a most complete and definitive manner; 2) God is judging us on our decision to accept or reject Jesus.

In the gospel passage for today, John states: "An hour is coming, has indeed come, when the dead shall hear the voice of the Son of God, and those who have heeded it shall live" (Jn 5:25). "Hearing the voice of Jesus" (Jn 5:25) means believing in Jesus. God judges us, even now, on whether or not we choose to believe in his Son's dying and rising. The "hour," which John describes, is happening right now. In fact, the hour of Jesus lasts forever, because the risen Jesus, present among us, is God's continuing offer of salvation to us.

When we were baptized, we expressed for the first time our decision to believe in Jesus. We committed ourselves to sharing in his death and Resurrection by dying to our selfishness and by becoming alive to God (Rom 6:3, 11). But baptism was not a private affair between one person and God. When we were baptized, we committed ourselves to love relationships within the Christian community.

In purgatory, the faithful departed are being purged of all selfishness which prohibits them from loving in their full capacity. A new kind of self-love replaces selfishness. The holy souls begin to recognize that God truly loves them in Jesus. In this awesome awareness, the soul then are able to respond wholeheartedly to God's love for them in Jesus.

Today we pray that the holy souls will reach that heavenly experience. In the Eucharist, we celebrate the "hour of Jesus," the continuing presence of the risen Lord among us. This same Jesus is here and now transforming the faithful departed into genuine lovers. We can support our brothers and sisters in purgatory by expressing in the Eucharist our commitment to become Jesus' community, people who are learning to love each other as Jesus loved us (Jn 13:34).

*The lectionary contains other readings which are optional for this feast.

November 9
THE DEDICATION OF THE LATERAN BASILICA

Rv 21:1–5
1 Cor 3:9–13, 16,17
Jn 2:13–22

Today we celebrate the Dedication of the Lateran Basilica, the Basilica of our Savior. The main purpose for a church building is to enable people to direct their minds and hearts to God in loving praise. And so this feast is not primarily concerned with a building: "Are you not aware that you are the temple of God, and that the Spirit of God dwells in you?" (1 Cor 3:16) The central theme in our liturgy today is the rededication of ourselves as a people intent on praising our Father. As God's people, alive in Jesus, we are "a new Jerusalem, the holy city" (Rv 21:2). "This is God's dwelling among men. He shall dwell with them and they shall be his people and he shall be their God who is always with them" (Rv 21:3).

In today's gospel, Jesus refers to himself as God's temple (Jn 2:19–22). Jesus is personally God's temple, because in him dwells the fulness of God. Jesus realized how unique was his love relationship with his Father. He knew his Father loved him so completely that, throughout his life, Jesus sought to return the Father's love. Finally, while dying, Jesus perfectly expressed his loving response to his Father.

Now as risen Lord, Jesus shares his Spirit with us. Since the Spirit of Jesus lives in our hearts, we are God's temple (1 Cor 3:16). We are able to share in the perfect act of worship which Jesus expressed on the cross. The risen Lord continues to express his full act of worship through us. This means that the center of worship is no longer a temple of stone in Jerusalem. We, God's people, are now able to worship in the Spirit of Jesus. We are God's living temple: "An hour is coming, and is already here, when authentic worshippers will worship the Father in Spirit and truth. Indeed, it is just such worshippers the Father seeks" (Jn 4:23).

Jesus is here among us today to lead us in our worship of the Father. We praise our Father in a manner which delights him—through Jesus, with Jesus, and in Jesus. "It is just such worshippers the Father seeks" (Jn 4:23). As we celebrate the Eucharist, we can rededicate ourselves as a people who are enthusiastic about praising our Father. Spirited in Jesus, we cry out: "Abba!" "Father!" (Gal 4:6).

THANKSGIVING DAY

Dt 8:7–18
Eph 1:3–14
Mk 5:18–20

Today throughout our nation we observe Thanksgiving Day, the special day on which we thank God for everything he has given us. As we prepare for the Eucharist, it is helpful to reflect on today's readings. In the readings, God reminds us that, of all his material and spiritual gifts, our greatest blessing is our love relationship with him. Through Jesus our brother, we are able to relate to God as our Father.

Even in the Old Testament, material prosperity was considered in the context of the Sinai covenant, the extraordinary love relationship between God and his people. God first invited the Israelites in the desert to respond to him with love and gratitude. God then invited each subsequent generation of Israelites to renew this same love relationship by recalling what God had done for their forefathers: "Be careful not to forget the LORD your God. . . . Otherwise, you might say to yourself, 'It is my own power . . . that has obtained for me this wealth'" (Dt 8:11, 17).

Through Jesus, the God of Israel has become our Father! This is God's greatest gift to us. None of us is so good and deserving that we need Jesus "less than" others need him. All of us need Jesus to be able to relate to God as our Father. Today's gospel helps us to express our gratitude to God. Jesus tells the man cured in the gospel: "Go home to your family and make it clear to them how much the Lord in his mercy has done for you" (Mk 5:19). Jesus now invites us to testify to each other how grateful we are for what God has done for us through Jesus.

The second reading also helps us praise our heavenly Father for the amazing blessings he has given to us through his Son (Eph 1:3-14). We are part of God's plan: "He . . . predestined us through Christ Jesus to be his adopted sons" (Eph 1:5). In heaven, we will all be united in Christ, our Savior (Eph 1:10, 14).

Today we gather to thank God for all his material and spiritual gifts to us. Jesus our brother is here with us to lead us in celebrating our meal of thanksgiving. We express our gratitude to God be recommitting ourselves to our covenant relationship with our Father. Through Jesus, we praise God with love in our hearts: "Praised be the God and Father of our Lord Jesus Christ, who has bestowed on us in Christ every spiritual blessing in the heavens!" (Eph 1:3).

The lectionary contains other readings that are optional for this day.